Tom Murphy

Alice Trilogy

In the Apiary

By the Gasworks Wall

At the Airport

Methuen Drama

Published by Methuen 2005

1 3 5 7 9 10 8 6 4 2

First published in 2005 by
Methuen Publishing Limited
11–12 Buckingham Gate
London SW1E 6LB

Methuen Publishing Limited Reg. No. 3543167

A CIP catalogue record for this book is available from
the British Library

ISBN 0 413 77576 3

Typeset by Country Setting, Kingsdown, Kent
Printed and bound in Great Britain by
Bookmarque Ltd, Croydon, Surrey

ROYAL COURT

Royal Court Theatre presents

ALICE TRILOGY
by **Tom Murphy**

First performance at The Royal Court Jerwood Theatre Downstairs
Sloane Square, London on 10 November 2005.

2005/06 ECO London Series

Thu 1 Dec 2005 at 7.30pm
Handel's Messiah
Christmas 2005

Wed 7 Dec 2005 at 7.30pm
Britten's St. Nicolas
Christmas 2005

ECO
05/06

Wed 14 Dec 2005 at 7.30pm
Berlioz's L'Enfance du Christ
Christmas 2005

English
Chamber
Orchestra

Wed 1 Feb 2006 at 7.30pm
Mozart's Requiem
Mozart 250

Forty-fifth
Anniversary
Season

Wed 22 Feb 2006 at 7.30pm
Gothoni and Noras
Schubert and Mahler

Sat 8 Apr 2006 at 7pm
Vladimir Ashkenazy
Mendelssohn and Strauss

Wed 24 May 2006 at 7.30pm
Emanuel Ax
Mozart 250

Cadogan Hall
Box Office:
020 7730 4500
www.cadoganhall.com

Save 10% when you book
tickets for any of the
Christmas concerts quoting
Royal Court offer

ALICE TRILOGY

by **Tom Murphy**

Cast in order of appearance
Alice **Juliet Stevenson**
Al/Waitress **Derbhle Crotty**
Jimmy/Waiter **Stanley Townsend**
Bundler/Official **Christopher Patrick Nolan**
Bill **John Stahl**

Director **Ian Rickson**
Designer **Jeremy Herbert**
Lighting Designer **Nigel Edwards**
Sound Designer **Ian Dickinson**
Composer **Stephen Warbeck**
Assistant Director **Elinna Männi**
Production Manager **Paul Handley**
Stage Manager **Tariq Sayyid Rifaat**
Deputy Stage Manager **Pippa Meyer**
Assistant Stage Manager **David Somers**
Stage Management Work Placement **Jessica Jeske**
Costume Supervisor **Iona Kenrick**
Dialect Coach **Joan Washington**
Company Voice Work **Patsy Rodenburg**
Set built by **Miraculous Engineering**

THE COMPANY

Tom Murphy (writer)
Tom Murphy is an award-winning writer whose long career was celebrated by the Abbey Theatre, Dublin, with a major retrospective of his work in 2001. His plays include The Drunkard, The House, The Wake, She Stoops to Folly, Famine, Too Late for Logic, The Morning After Optimism, The Sanctuary Lamp, Bailegangaire, The Gigli Concert, Conversations on a Homecoming and A Whistle in the Dark.

Derbhle Crotty
At the Royal Court: Portia Coughlan (& Peacock, Dublin); The Weir (tour).
Other theatre includes: The Home Place (Gate, Dublin/Comedy,West End); Dancing at Lughnasa (Gate, Dublin); Sive, The Good Father (Druid/Olypia/Gaeity/tour); The Plough and the Stars, The Well of the Saints, (Abbey, Dublin); Royal Supreme (Theatre Royal, Plymouth); The Playboy of the Western World, Summerfolk, The Merchant of Venice (RNT); Little Eyolf, Camino Real, Hamlet (RSC); Portia Coughlan, The Mai Beauty in a Broken Place, Bailegangaire, Kaite Roche (Peacock, Dublin); Playing the Wife (Chichester Festival/tour); Miss Julie (Andrew's Lane Theatre); Sandra/Manon (Dublin Festival); Measure for Measure (Galloglass Theatre Company).
Television includes: Any Time Now, Poorhouse, Gold in the Streets.
Film Includes: Notes On A Scandal, Inside I'm Dancing.
Radio includes: Weight of Water, Quinn, St. Patrick's Daughter.
Awards include: Ian Charleston Award 1997.

Ian Dickinson (sound designer)
For the Royal Court: Fewer Emergencies, Way to Heaven, The Woman Before, Stoning Mary (& Drum Theatre, Plymouth), Breathing Corpses, Wild East, Shining City (& Gate, Dublin), Lucky Dog, Blest Be the Tie (with Talawa), Ladybird, Notes on Falling Leaves, Loyal Women, The Sugar Syndrome, Blood, Playing the Victim (with Told By an Idiot), Fallout, Flesh Wound, Hitchcock Blonde (& Lyric), Black Milk, Crazyblackmuthafuckin'self, Caryl Churchill Shorts, Push Up, Fucking Games, Herons.
Other theatre includes: Port, As You Like It, Poor Superman, Martin Yesterday, Fast Food, Coyote Ugly (Royal Exchange, Manchester); Night of the Soul (RSC/Barbican); Eyes of the Kappa (Gate); Crime & Punishment in Dalston (Arcola); Search & Destroy (New End); The Whore's Dream (RSC/Edinburgh).
Ian is Head of Sound at the Royal Court.

Nigel Edwards (lighting designer)
For the Royal Court: Stoning Mary, Ladybird, Flesh Wound (Galway Festival); Fallout, 4.48 Psychosis, Cleansed, Crave (Paines Plough/Bright Ltd tour); Bailengangaire (Ambassadors).
Other theatre includes: When Harry Met Sally (Haymarket); Sexual Perversity in Chicago (Comedy); The Postman Always Rings Twice (Playhouse); The Oresteia (RNT); The Tempest (European/UK tour); Victoria, Roberto Zucco, The Mysteries, Shadows (RSC); Splendour, Riddance, Sleeping Around (with Salisbury Playhouse), The Cosmonaut's Last Message (Paines Plough); The Triumph of Love (Almeida/UK tour); The Maids; (Young Vic); Colder Than Here, Flush, Dirty Butterfly (Soho/UK tour); The Misanthrope (Gate, Dublin); Romeo & Juliet (Cork/Athlone/Dublin); Pigg in Hell, Total Massala Slammer, The Anderson Project, Portraits (Remote Control); Clare de Luz (Insomniac); Inconceivable, Mister Heracles (West Yorkshire Playhouse); One Minute, Arabian Night, The Boy Who Left Home (Actors Touring Company); Bloody Mess, Disco Relax, The Voices, First NIght, Pleasure, Showtime, Speak Bitterness, Hidden J., Club of No Regrets, Emmanuelle Enchanted, Mania and Lee (Forced Entertainment); Girl in the Goldfishbowl (Sheffield Crucible).
Opera includes: Jenufa (Welsh National Opera), The Maids (Lyric); Hansel & Gretel (Opera North). He designs and tours extensively with Forced Entertainment, The Right Size and Tottering Bipeds. He designed the lighting for productions at the Welsh National Opera and the Lyric Hammersmith.

Jeremy Herbert (designer)
For the Royal Court; Thyestes, Ashes and Sand, The Lights, Cleansed, 4.48 Psychosis (Barclay's Best Design Award).
Other stage designs include; This is Our Youth (Garrick); Up For Grabs - starring Madonna (Wyndham's); Sexual Perversity in Chicago (Haymarket); The Tempest, Roberto Zucco, Beauty and the Beast (RSC); Attempts on her Life, (Piccolo Teatro, Milan); The Triumph of Love (Almeida); and the premiere of John Taverner's opera Mary of Egypt at the Aldeburgh Festival.
As a multimedia artist recent projects include: collaborations with Artangel - Imber (Salisbury Plain) and Michael Nyman, Man and Boy DADA - (Almeida/USA).
Last year he was awarded a NESTA Dreamtime Fellowship with which to develop his work.

Elina Männi (assistant director)
As assistant director for the Royal Court: Harvest.
As a director theatre includes: Our Little Destabilisation (Camden People's Theatre); Vagina Monologues (Ugala Repertory Theatre, Estonia); Machinal (White Bear); Dossier: Ronald Akkerman (Finborough); Funnyhouse of a Negro, Gone Out (Rose Bruford); Mouthful of Birds (SFA Downstage

Theater, USA); Streetwise (Union); Euston Language (King's Head); Rainbow Conversations (Arcola). Elina is currently trainee director on attachment at Royal Court, with support of the Channel 4 Theatre Directors' Scheme Bursary (sponsored by the Harold Hyam Wingate Foundation).

Christopher Patrick Nolan
Theatre Includes: Stones in his Pockets (New Ambassadors/national tour); Molly Sweeney (Theatre Clwyd/national tour), Someone Who'll Watch Over Me (Palace Theatre, Westcliff/national tour), Antigone (Sheffield Crucible/national tour); The Changeling, Of Mice and Men (Southwark Playhouse); Into The West/Tir Na n'Og (Harbourfront Centre, Toronto and USA tour); The Romans In Britain (Man in the Moon); Macbeth, Othello (Riverside Studios); Cardenio (Globe); The Canterbury Tales (Edinburgh Festival); Cloud Nine (Lyric, Hammersmith); King Lear (West Yorkshire Playhouse).
Television includes: Titanic Birth of a Legend.
Film includes: That Deadwood Feeling, Lone Clouds.

Ian Rickson (director)
For the Royal Court: The Sweetest Swing in Baseball, Fallout, The Night Heron, Boy Gets Girl, Mouth to Mouth (& Albery), Dublin Carol, The Weir (Duke of York's/Broadway), The Lights, Pale Horse, Mojo (& Steppenwolf Theatre, Chicago), Ashes & Sand, Some Voices, Killers (1992 Young Writers Festival), Wildfire.
Other theatre includes: The Day I Stood Still (RNT); The House of Yes (Gate, London); Me and My Friend (Chichester Festival Theatre); Queer Fish (BAC); First Strike (Soho Poly).
Opera includes: La Serva Padrona (Broomhill).
Ian Rickson is Artistic Director at the Royal Court.

John Stahl
For the Royal Court: The Weir.
Other theatre includes: Blue Eyes and Heels, Angels and Saints (Soho); The Found Man, Gagarin Way, Anna Weiss, Shining Souls, The Architect (Traverse); Mr. Placebo (Traverse/Plymouth); The Meeting (Traverse/Edinburgh); Professor Bernhardi (OSC/Dumbfounded); Serjeant Musgrave's Dance, Bread and Butter (OSC); Tamar's Revenge, Dog In The Manger, Pedro, The Great Pretender (RSC); Crave (Paines Plough); The Magic Toyshop (Shared Experience); All My Sons (Theatre Royal Plymouth); Two (Cumbernauld Theatre Co.); The Jock Stein Story (Pavilion, Glasgow); Hamlet (Belgrade, Coventry); Cinderella (Dundee Rep.) The Real World, The Baby, Paddy's Market, Sleeping Beauty, Gamblers, Macbeth (Tron); The Crucible, The Snow Queen, Death of a Salesman (Lyceum Edinburgh); Beneath One Banner (7:84); Commedia (Sheffield Crucible/Lyric Hammersmith/

Scottish Theatre Co.); The Midas Plays (Brian Way's); The Glass Menagerie, The Caretaker, What the Butler Saw, Entertaining Mr. Sloane, Zoo Story, School For Clowns (Cumbernauld Theatre Co.).
Radio includes: Gagarin Way, Macleavy, The Laughing Policeman.
As Assistant director: Darlington Drama Centre 1975-6, The Sash, The Game, Willie The Wonderful Wizard (Cumbernauld Theatre Co.).
Awards Include: The Stage Award for Acting Excellence 1997, (Traverse Theatre Production Edinburgh Festival Fringe).

Juliet Stevenson
For the Royal Court: The Country, Death and the Maiden, Other Worlds.
Other theatre includes: Beckett Shorts, Les Liaisons Dangereuses, As You Like It, Troilus and Cressida, Measure for Measure, A Midsummer Night's Dream, The Witch of Edmonton, Money, Henry IV Parts I and II, Once in a Lifetime, The White Guard, Hippolytus, Antony and Cleopatra, The Churchill Play, The Taming of the Shrew, The Tempest (RSC); We Happy Few (Gielgud); Private Lives, Hedda Gabler, Yerma (RNT); The Caucasian Chalk Circle (Complicité/RNT); The Trackers of Oxyrhynchus (National Studio); The Duchess of Malfi (Greenwich/West End); Death and the Maiden (Duke of York's); Scenes from an Execution (Mark Taper Forum LA); On The Verge (Sadler's Wells); Burn This (Hampstead/Lyric).
Television includes: Pierrepoint, Hear the Silence, The Pact, Trial By Fire, Cider With Rosie, Stone Scissors Paper, The Politician's Wife, Out of Love, Stanley, Life Story, Antigone, Freud, Bazaar and Rummage, The Mallens, Maybury, Oedipus At Colonus, Great Journeys Isabelle Eberhardt.
Film includes: Every Word Is True, Red Mercury Rising, Being Julia, Mona Lisa Smile, Nicholas Nickleby, Food of Love, Bend It Like Beckham, The Search for John Gissing, The Road from Coorain, Play, Emma, A Secret Rapture, Who Dealt, The Trial, Truly, Madly, Deeply, Ladder of Swords, Drowning By Numbers, Volcano, Who's Afraid of Virginia Woolf, The Pallisers, Man and Superman.
Radio includes: Hang Up, Whale Music, Cigarettes and Chocolate, A Little Like Drowning.
Awards include: Drama Magazine Best Actress Award for Measure for Measure, Ace Cable TV Network Best Supporting Actress Award for Life Story, Time Out Best Actress Award, Laurence Olivier Best Actress Award for Death and the Maiden, Emmy Best Children's Film for Television Award for Living With Dinosaurs, LA Drama Critics Circle Best Actress Award for Scenes from an Execution, Australian Film Institute, Best Actress in a Television Drama Award for The Road from Corrain, Evening Standard Film Award Best Actress, for Truly Madly Deeply.

Stanley Townsend

For Royal Court: Shining City, Under the Blue Sky. Other theatre includes: Remember This, Guys & Dolls, The Little Clay Cart (RNT); The Weir (Duke of York's/Australian tour); The Gingerbread Mix Up (Andrew's Lane, Dublin); Amphibians (Dublin Festival); The Wake, Trinity for Two, Sacred Mysteries (Abbey, Dublin); Art (Wyndhams Theatre); Prayers of Sherkin (Old Vic); Who Shall Be Happy? (Mad Cow tour); Pride & Prejudice, Oleanna, The Dream, The Double Dealer, The Cherry Orchard (Gate Theatre Dublin); Democracy (Bush); Speed-the-Plow (Project Arts); Someone to Watch Over Me (West Yorkshire Playhouse); The Plough & the Stars (Young Vic); Saint Oscar (Field Day); Sexual Perversity in Chicago, The Caucasian Chalk Circle, The Country Wife, Nightshade, The White Devil (Rough Magic); I Can't Get Started (Dublin/ Edinburgh Festival). Television includes: Spooke, Elizabeth the Virgin Queen, Omagh Bombing, The Brief, Murder Squad, Fallen, Wire in the Blood, The Commander, Seventh Stream, Menace, Heartbeat, Station Jim, Table 12, Casualty, Best of Both Worlds, Active Defence, DDU, Ballykissangel, Peak Practice, Jonathan Creek, A Touch of Frost, Career Opportunities, Bliss, The Governor, The Bill, Parnell, Nighthawks, Fortycoats, Lost Belongings, Lapsed Catholics, Glenroe. Film includes: The Libertine, Isolation, Inside I'm Dancing, Tulse Luper II, Suzie Gold, Wondrous Oblivion, American Girl, Monsieur N, Mystics, The Van, My Friend Joe, Moll Flanders, Jake's Progress, Beyond Reason, Good Girls, In the Name of the Father, Blue Ice, Into the West, The Miracle, Taffin.

Stanley is a founding member of Rough Magic Theatre Company.

Awards include; Irish Times and nomination for the Evening Standard Award 2004 (for Shining City).

Stephen Warbeck (composer)

For the Royal Court: Fallout, The Night Heron, Boy Gets Girl, Mouth to Mouth (and West End), Dublin Carol, The Glory of Living, The Lights, Harry and Me, Pale Horse, Rat in the Skull, Mojo, Simpatico, The Editing Process, The Kitchen, Blood, Greenland, Bloody Poetry, A Lie of the Mind, Built on Sand.

Other theatre includes: Pericles, Prince of Tyre (Globe); Proof, To the Green Fields Beyond (Donmar); Alice in Wonderland, Romeo and Juliet, The Tempest, Cymbeline, The Cherry Orchard (RSC/Albery/national tour); The Villian's Opera, The Prime of Miss Jean Brodie, The Day I Stood Still, Light Shining in Buckinghamshire, Machinal, At Our Table (RNT); An Inspector Calls (RNT/West End, Broadway/Japan/Australia/Vienna).

Films include: Feast of the Goat, Cargo, Travaux, On a Clear Day, Mickybo & Me, Two Brothers, Oyster Farmer, Proof, De Zaak Alzheimer, Pour Le Plaisir, Love's Brother, Blackball, Mystics, Charlotte Gray, Birthday Girl, Captain Corelli's Mandolin, Gabriel and Me, Billy Elliot, Quills, Very Annie Mary, Mystery Men, Fanny and Elvis, Shakespeare in Love, Heart, Mrs Brown, My Son the Fanatic, Brothers in Trouble, Different for Girls, Sister My Sister, O Mary This London.

Awards include: Academy Award and BAFTA nomination for Best Original Musical or Comedy Score for Shakespeare in Love, 2001 ASCAP Award for Best Film Music for Quills.

Stephen also writes for his band the hKippers and for The Metropolitan Water Board. His first ballet commission was for Peter Pan (Northern Ballet/Sadlers Wells);

THE ENGLISH STAGE COMPANY AT THE ROYAL COURT

The English Stage Company at the Royal Court opened in 1956 as a subsidised theatre producing new British plays, international plays and some classical revivals.

The first artistic director George Devine aimed to create a writers' theatre, 'a place where the dramatist is acknowledged as the fundamental creative force in the theatre and where the play is more important than the actors, the director, the designer'. The urgent need was to find a contemporary style in which the play, the acting, direction and design are all combined. He believed that 'the battle will be a long one to continue to create the right conditions for writers to work in'.

Devine aimed to discover 'hard-hitting, uncompromising writers whose plays are stimulating, provocative and exciting'. The Royal Court production of John Osborne's Look Back in Anger in May 1956 is now seen as the decisive starting point of modern British drama and the policy created a new generation of British playwrights. The first wave included John Osborne, Arnold Wesker, John Arden, Ann Jellicoe, N F Simpson and Edward Bond. Early seasons included new international plays by Bertolt Brecht, Eugène Ionesco, Samuel Beckett, Jean-Paul Sartre and Marguerite Duras.

The theatre started with the 400-seat proscenium arch Theatre Downstairs, and in 1969 opened a second theatre, the 60-seat studio Theatre Upstairs. Some productions transfer to the West End, such as Terry Johnson's Hitchcock Blonde, Caryl Churchill's Far Away and Conor McPherson's The Weir. Recent touring productions include Sarah Kane's 4.48 Psychosis (US tour) and Ché Walker's Flesh Wound (Galway Arts Festival). The Royal Court also co-produces plays which transfer to the West End or tour internationally, such as Conor McPherson's Shining City (with Gate Theatre, Dublin), Sebastian Barry's The Steward of Christendom and Mark Ravenhill's Shopping and Fucking (with Out of Joint), Martin McDonagh's The Beauty Queen of Leenane (with Druid), Ayub Khan Din's East is East (with Tamasha).

Since 1994 the Royal Court's artistic policy has again been vigorously directed to finding and producing a new generation of playwrights. The writers include Joe Penhall, Rebecca Prichard, Michael Wynne, Nick Grosso, Judy Upton, Meredith Oakes, Sarah Kane, Anthony Neilson, Judith Johnson, James Stock, Jez Butterworth, Marina Carr, Phyllis Nagy, Simon Block, Martin

photo: Andy Chopping

McDonagh, Mark Ravenhill, Ayub Khan Din, Tamantha Hammerschlag, Jess Walters, Ché Walker, Conor McPherson, Simon Stephens, Richard Bean, Roy Williams, Gary Mitchell, Mick Mahoney, Rebecca Gilman, Christopher Shinn, Kia Corthron, David Gieselmann, Marius von Mayenburg, David Eldridge, Leo Butler, Zinnie Harris, Grae Cleugh, Roland Schimmelpfennig, Chloe Moss, DeObia Oparei, Enda Walsh, Vassily Sigarev, the Presnyakov Brothers, Marcos Barbosa, Lucy Prebble, John Donnelly, Clare Pollard, Robin French, Elyzabeth Gregory Wilder, Rob Evans, Laura Wade and Debbie Tucker Green. This expanded programme of new plays has been made possible through the support of A.S.K. Theater Projects and the Skirball Foundation, The Jerwood Charity, the American Friends of the Royal Court Theatre and (in 1994/5 and 1999) in association with the National Theatre Studio.

In recent years there have been record-breaking productions at the box office, with capacity houses for Joe Penhall's Dumb Show, Conor McPherson's Shining City, Roy Williams' Fallout and Terry Johnson's Hitchcock Blonde.

The refurbished theatre in Sloane Square opened in February 2000, with a policy still inspired by the first artistic director George Devine. The Royal Court is an international theatre for new plays and new playwrights, and the work shapes contemporary drama in Britain and overseas.

AWARDS FOR
THE ROYAL COURT

jez Butterworth won the 1995 George Devine Award, the Writers' Guild New Writer of the Year Award, the Evening Standard Award for Most Promising Playwright and the Olivier Award for Best Comedy for Mojo.

The Royal Court was the overall winner of the 1995 Prudential Award for the Arts for creativity, excellence, innovation and accessibility. The Royal Court Theatre Upstairs won the 1995 Peter Brook Empty Space Award for innovation and excellence in theatre.

Michael Wynne won the 1996 Meyer-Whitworth Award for The Knocky. Martin McDonagh won the 1996 George Devine Award, the 1996 Writers' Guild Best Fringe Play Award, the 1996 Critics' Circle Award and the 1996 Evening Standard Award for Most Promising Playwright for The Beauty Queen of Leenane. Marina Carr won the 19th Susan Smith Blackburn Prize (1996/7) for Portia Coughlan. Conor McPherson won the 1997 George Devine Award, the 1997 Critics' Circle Award and the 1997 Evening Standard Award for Most Promising Playwright for The Weir. Ayub Khan Din won the 1997 Writers' Guild Awards for Best West End Play and New Writer of the Year and the 1996 John Whiting Award for East is East (co-production with Tamasha).

Martin McDonagh's The Beauty Queen of Leenane (co-production with Druid Theatre Company) won four 1998 Tony Awards including Garry Hynes for Best Director. Eugene Ionesco's The Chairs (co-production with Theatre de Complicite) was nominated for six Tony awards. David Hare won the 1998 Time Out Live Award for Outstanding Achievement and six awards in New York including the Drama League, Drama Desk and New York Critics Circle Award for Via Dolorosa. Sarah Kane won the 1998 Arts Foundation Fellowship in Playwriting. Rebecca Prichard won the 1998 Critics' Circle Award for Most Promising Playwright for Yard Gal (co-production with Clean Break).

Conor McPherson won the 1999 Olivier Award for Best New Play for The Weir. The Royal Court won the 1999 ITI Award for Excellence in International Theatre. Sarah Kane's Cleansed was judged Best Foreign Language Play in 1999 by Theater Heute in Germany. Gary Mitchell won the 1999 Pearson Best Play Award for Trust. Rebecca Gilman was joint winner of the 1999 George Devine Award and won the 1999 Evening Standard Award for Most Promising Playwright for The Glory of Living.

In 1999, the Royal Court won the European theatre prize New Theatrical Realities, presented at Taormina Arte in Sicily, for its efforts in recent years in discovering and producing the work of young British dramatists.

Roy Williams and Gary Mitchell were joint winners of the George Devine Award 2000 for Most Promising Playwright for Lift Off and The Force of Change respectively. At the Barclays Theatre Awards 2000 presented by the TMA, Richard Wilson won the Best Director Award for David Gieselmann's Mr Kolpert and Jeremy Herbert won the Best Designer Award for Sarah Kane's 4.48 Psychosis. Gary Mitchell won the Evening Standard's Charles Wintour Award 2000 for Most Promising Playwright for The Force of Change. Stephen Jeffreys' I Just Stopped by to See the Man won an AT&T: On Stage Award 2000.

David Eldridge's Under the Blue Sky won the Time Out Live Award 2001 for Best New Play in the West End. Leo Butler won the George Devine Award 2001 for Most Promising Playwright for Redundant. Roy Williams won the Evening Standard's Charles Wintour Award 2001 for Most Promising Playwright for Clubland. Grae Cleugh won the 2001 Olivier Award for Most Promising Playwright for Fucking Games. Richard Bean was joint winner of the George Devine Award 2002 for Most Promising Playwright for Under the Whaleback. Caryl Churchill won the 2002 Evening Standard Award for Best New Play for A Number. Vassily Sigarev won the 2002 Evening Standard Charles Wintour Award for Most Promising Playwright for Plasticine. Ian MacNeil won the 2002 Evening Standard Award for Best Design for A Number and Plasticine. Peter Gill won the 2002 Critics' Circle Award for Best New Play for The York Realist (English Touring Theatre). Ché Walker won the 2003 George Devine Award for Most Promising Playwright for Flesh Wound. Lucy Prebble won the 2003 Critics' Circle Award and the 2004 George Devine Award for Most Promising Playwright, and the TMA Theatre Award 2004 for Best New Play for The Sugar Syndrome. Linda Bassett won the 2004 TMA Theatre Award for Best Actress (for Leo Butler's Lucky Dog).

ROYAL COURT BOOKSHOP

The Royal Court bookshop offers a range of contemporary plays and publications on the theory and practice of modern drama. The staff specialise in assisting with the selection of audition monologues and scenes. Royal Court playtexts from past and present productions cost £2.
The Bookshop is situated in the downstairs
ROYAL COURT BAR
Monday–Friday 3–10pm, Saturday 2.30–10pm
For information tel: 020 7565 5024
or email: bookshop@royalcourttheatre.com

PROGRAMME SUPPORTERS

The Royal Court (English Stage Company Ltd) receives its principal funding from Arts Council England, London. It is also supported financially by a wide range of private companies, charitable and public bodies, and earns the remainder of its income from the box office and its own trading activities.

The Genesis Foundation supports International Playwrights and the Young Writers' Festival. The Jerwood Charity supports new plays by new playwrights through the Jerwood New Playwrights series.

The Skirball Foundation funds a Playwrights' Programme at the theatre. The Artistic Director's Chair is supported by a lead grant from The Peter Jay Sharp Foundation, contributing to the activities of the Artistic Director's office. Bloomberg Mondays, the Royal Court's reduced price ticket scheme, is supported by Bloomberg. Over the past eight years the BBC has supported the Gerald Chapman Fund for directors.

ROYAL COURT
SLOANE SQUARE

**7– 22 December
Jerwood Theatre Upstairs**

The Contact Theatre, Manchester
production of

WHAT'S IN THE CAT
by **Linda Brogan**

Lauren's come back for Christmas dinner, but she's not staying. They've found her a place with a creche so she can do her exams. Dad thinks she should have kept her legs shut. It's Moss Side, 1974.

director **Paulette Randall**
design **Libby Watson**
lighting design **James Farncombe**

cast include: **Rachel Brogan,
Curtis Cole**

12 January–11 February 2006

Jerwood Theatre Downstairs

Royal Court and Out of Joint
present

O GO MY MAN
by **Stella Feehily**

director **Max Stafford-Clark**
designer **Es Devlin**
lighting **Johanna Town**
sound **Gareth Fry**

cast includes: **Paul Hickey,
Denise Gough, Sam Graham,
Susan Lynch, Aoife McMahon,
Gemma Reeves**

BOX OFFICE
020 7565 5000
BOOK ONLINE
www.royalcourttheatre.com

For Nell

with love

In the Apiary

Characters

Alice
Al

Time: the eighties.

A shaft of light cuts downwards through the murk (as it might, coming from a dormer window or skylight); its spill distinguishes — but does not quite clearly define — a few objects of broken furniture, including a cheval mirror that stands somewhat askew. A second light, a narrow swathe (as from a landing outside a door, the door ajar) cuts a path into this space. A continuous sound, not very loud, ascended from below, hangs here. (Hard to know what it is, though it is a radio.)

Something that sounds like the chirrup of a bird, outside. A beat or two and it comes again: the lonely chirrup of a solitary bird.

Another sound is ascending to join the first — a remote thump-thump, thump-thump, continuous. (A washing machine engaging with the radio.) Strange little world up here.

The swathe of light across the floor widens and **Alice** *comes in, soft-shoed, silently; fast rather than slow, but neither. (Like a rat on a familiar run that believes itself to be unobserved, that looks neither left nor right, making for a familiar stopping place? Perhaps.) En route, now, she stops. She is like a woman with a continuous headache. She's forgotten something, has she? Or what has she to do that has made her stop?*

Alice Yes? . . . Yes.

And she returns the path she came to close the door, to shut out the sounds from down below; and the swathe of light across the floor, too, is killed.

On her way again, she stops again, and:

Yes? . . . What? . . . Oh, yes.

She has pills in her fist; she takes them — two pills: her action is awkward, the fist appearing to rub the mouth upwards. (Like a rat again, pushing a grain of corn into its mouth.) All the time, from entering, she has been carrying a cup and saucer in one hand.

She has found her stopping place. She sips from the cup.

Hello? (*Sips.*) Yes? (*Sips.*) Anybody home? (*Taps her head.*) No one at home. Good.

Alice *is in her twenties. Long dress of a young woman. (Perhaps an Arab-type dress with the square of bodice hand-embroidered.)*

She produces a bottle of whisky from a hiding place. She laces the cup, and sips.

While she does this, a figure emerges gradually from the darkness behind her, a young woman like herself, to stand framed in the mirror and eventually to step out of it. **Alice** *is refusing to/does not acknowledge her. (The figure is called* **Al**.*)*

Al   Your name, age and profession, please?

Alice   Out to lunch. (*Meaning 'crazy', as earlier with 'No one at home'.*)

Al   And that is a good start to our programme today. Okay, hockay, alrighty, we're off! And here is your starter for two – start the clock! Who wrote – ?

Alice   . . . What?

Al   *Hamlet.*

Alice   Stupid.

Al   No-o! I'll give you a clue then. He also wrote *Romeo and* – ?

Alice   Jeeeezzzstupid. (*She sips to make more room in the cup for a bigger lacing. She puts the bottle away.*)

Al   But let her settle herself first, do whatever she is doing to her coffee first, then any question you like, she'll give you the answer, now she's away from that room down there.

Alice   Yeah. (*Agreeing with the last clause.*)

Al   Supply the missing word in the title of this song.

Alice   Christ.

Al   No-o! I haven't given you the question yet. The missing word in the title of this song: 'The Green, Green' *what* 'of Home'.

Alice   Christ.

Al   'Green, Green' what 'of Home' – Running out of time – What would Tom Jones like to feel, what would Tom Jones like to touch?

Alice *is shaking her head, saying 'Christ' to herself and perhaps even smiling at the persistence of inanities, and she produces cigarettes.*

Al   But let her light a cigarette first, sit down and take her ease first, now that she's got?

Alice   Twenty-five minutes. (*With a glance at her watch.*)

Al   Before collecting the children from school. So, 'The Green, Green' what 'of Home'?

Alice (*puffs*)   How green is your Valium? (*Sips.*) Start again.

Al   State your name.

Alice   My name is Alice − I think.

Al   Hockay, Alice! So, let me see −

Alice   Decent questions.

Al   Decent questions, start again, come again.

Alice   *Recommencer, encore une fois?*

Al   . . . Oh! I see! Very good, *very* good.

Alice   *Une fois de plus, je comprends, très bien.*

Al   So, the Loreto education was *not* wasted.

Alice *sighs.*

Al   It's just that she's upset.

Alice   At the *moment* she's upset.

Al   And it's just that she cannot think what it is exactly is upsetting her at the moment.

Alice   One of those days as like as not.

Al   *Another* of those days as like as not.

Alice   . . . Yeah. (*'Another' of those days worries her a bit.*)

Al   She'll be fine in a little.

Alice   Will she?

Al   It stands to reason.

Alice   Will she?

Al   It *doesn't* stand to reason.

Alice   She'll be fine.

Al   Stands to reason! I mean and for instance, ask her would she be another housewife on the phone, talking to that concerned DJ over the radio and breaking down and she'll tell you – ?

Alice   What will she tell you? (*A bit of fear; it worries her.*)

Al   I'll tell you what she'll tell you. Let Big Al, her best pal, tell you what she'll tell you. She will tell, I'd be fucked first.

Alice (*relieved*)   Yeah.

Al   I mean – what?! – Radio people?! –

Alice   I ask you – !

Al   All of them sounding like –

Alice   Like –

Al   Fucking – !

Alice   Lay doctors –

Al   Lay doctors – !

Alice   Talking to the terminally ill.

Al   For fuck's sake! (*Then:*) Fucking –

Alice   Amateurs.

Al   Amateurs!

Alice   Don't be so stupid –

Al   She'd die at the thought.

Alice   Yeah. (*Relieved.*)

Al   Die at it.

Alice (*nods*) Yeah.

Al . . . A quiz show?

Alice Maybe.

Al Yes?

Alice Perhaps.

Al But the other thing?

Alice Don't make me laugh, chiphhh!

Al Don't make her laugh, chiphhh!

Al What do the following have in common: John the Baptist and Marilyn Monroe?

Alice Neither of them wore any?

Al Correct. (*Beat:*) She smokes.

Alice That's true.

Al A lot?

Alice I do.

Al And pills?

Alice A few.

Al A few, a few?

Alice And − ! (*Holding up her cup to declare that she drinks.*) That's true, but better than breaking down on the phone over the radio to a concerned DJ? (*She sips.*)

Al And her drinking's becoming hardly a secret.

Alice 'Cept!

Al 'Cept! Except to Big Bill.

Alice Wonder boy.

Al Her hubby. Who works in the bank, studies four nights a week, is in line for promotion and breeds budgies out there.

They listen for a sound of the birds.

Not a peep.

Alice (*listening to 'downstairs'*)   But he's still at it down there.

Al   Switch him off.

Alice   Talking to the terminally ill.

Al   Break his mouth for him, get a hammer, smash the set.

Alice   And listen to the washing machine?

Al   You have a point.

Alice   Or listen to you all day?

Al   *Another* point.

Alice   I'm not very keen on you, yeh know.

Al   I couldn't agree with you more. However, we must soldier on. Who died, who died, hum-haw, hum-haw, 'xactly hundred years ago today?

Alice   Jeezzzstupid.

Al   Shall I repeat the question?

Alice   No. Emily Brontë, Brian Boru, Princess Di, Beatrix Potter, Nelson Mandela, Winnie Mandela, Pope John the Twenty-whatever-you're-havin'-yourself and Mixtrix Quixley.

Al   Correct. Why do women have small feet?

Alice   But the person sitting here is not ill, short-term, terminally or otherwise: ask her. She is alive and she is of sound, sound mind. Ask her.

Al   I ask her.

Alice   I do not like the Pope, for instance?

Al *nods.*

Alice   And though I am prepared to believe that he loses no sleep over that fact – hmm?

Al *nods.*

Alice And though I am prepared to believe that the same lump of a man is a very sound sleeper – hmm?

Al Nevertheless?

Alice *nods.*

Al You don't like him.

Alice I don't like the man.

Al Nothing now against the Poles, mind you, have you?

Alice What could I have against the – ?!

Al Nothing racist.

Alice But.

Al His Holiness?

Alice Yeh. Penchant for skull-caps and kissing the ground?

Al Yet he won't look at a woman or wear a condom.

Alice It begs a question of sanity –

Al Faaack – !

Alice Let alone infallibility.

Al The 'Pontiff'.

Alice The 'Pontiff'.

Al Faaaaaaack! (*Laughing.*)

The title 'Pontiff' appears to be a source of amusement to them, and not for the first time it would seem, and they are laughing. **Alice** *pulls herself back; she's not playing.*

Alice No.

Al Yes! Don't stop now. Speaking of tits!

Alice No.

Al Twelve nineteens?

Alice   Two hundred and twenty-eight.

Al   Speaking of tits –

Alice   No, no –

Al   Ah, come on.

Alice   No, no –

Al   Speaking of tits –

Alice   I'm in bad humour –

Al   Speaking of tits, speaking of tits, yes – (*Pointing.*) Marco Polo?

Alice   No.

Al   Marco Polo who lives next door is . . . ? Is a queer – ?

Alice   Fish.

Al   Spends lot of time in his garden since he . . . ? Since he took early . . . ?

Alice   Confinement.

Al   She means retirement.

Alice (*sharply*)   I mean exactly what I say – always.

Al (*agrees*)   Well, lately he has started to dye his hair.

Alice   You hardly ever see Puddin, his wife, any more.

Al   But.

Alice   He's a queer fish all right: those eyes.

Al   But this day last month –

Alice (*sharply*)   Exactly to the day if I wish to say so.

Al (*agrees*)   He came to talk to her over the back-garden fence?

Alice *nods.*

Al   Ostensibly about Bill's budgies. (*Out there.*)

Alice   Well! (*Mild exclamation.*)

Al   Well! Just for fun she stooped down –

Alice   Ostensibly to pick a dandelion –

Al   But really to see what would happen –

Alice   And let one of her tits pop out of its cup.

Al   Well! Well, his fish-eyes got a start.

Alice   Well, they must have done.

Al   Because he left them there –

Alice   Foolishly –

Al   While the rest of him got out of it –

Alice   To crouch to a flowerbed on his side of the fence –

Al   Catching his cheek on a rose bush en route.

Alice   Iff! (*Baring her teeth in a wince.*)

Al   She met his startled eyes through a chink in the fence, tucked the tit back to where it lived, and –

Alice   Iff – !

Al   Winced again like Humphrey Bogart at the ruby of blood on his – (*Touching her cheek*). Hmm?

Alice *has drifted/is drifting away. She's thinking of something else – long ago/a time when she was free/whatever – other than 'Marco Polo'. Something wistful:*

Alice   And though he's not out there now . . . in this precious moment in time . . . precious moment in time . . .

Al   He's out there a lot in his garden since.

A chirrup from outside goes unacknowledged by them. **Alice** *is just looking at her cup.*

Al   It's just that she's upset, at the moment she's upset, and she cannot think what it is exactly is – *smash something*! – is upsetting her at the moment.

On 'smash something' **Alice***'s face became suddenly animated as in the consideration of a violent action, but she manages to contain the thought and, instead, gets the whisky bottle again and pours a measure into her cup.*

Al   *Du? Plus? Non-non, madame* –

Alice   *Oui!*

Al   *Non* – *non* –

Alice   *S'il vous plaît?*

Al   Hockay!

Alice   *Merci!* (*She puts the bottle away.*)

Al   Top of the class at school, weren't you, love?

Alice *qualifies this with a gesture/grimace.*

Al   Damn near. And as for the subject general knowledge?

Alice *nods/thumbs up.*

Al   Now called something else, of course.

Alice   Civics.

Al   So, my friends, you see who you're dealing with?

Alice *holds up a finger.*

Al (*in response*)   For instance: that – bird-house – out there –

Alice   I know that it's an aviary –

Al   But ask her, go on, ask her and she'll tell you.

Alice   I prefer to call it an apiary.

Al   She calls things what she likes.

Alice   Should I call things by what other people have decided for me?

Al   Her mind, her life.

Alice   My mind, my life.

Al Apiary.

Alice An apiary. For budgies and canaries and, and –
Doesn't matter.

Al She prefers to call them doesn't matter.

Alice Yeah. (*She drinks. She thinks.*)

Al But their singing all together, early in the morning,
creates a racket. (*She listens for a sound of the birds. Nothing.*)
Curiously, for the rest of the day they are quiet enough in
their wire-mesh and timber dwelling. Except, yes, for the
occasional outburst, for reasons best known or unknown to
themselves.

Alice Curiously, they are not all that gone on sunshine.
Coloured birds, yeh know?

Al Preferring the darkness of the dorm. Where, one
supposes, they screw one another like rattlesnakes.

Alice If rattlesnakes are silent whilst screwing, that is . . .
Hmm? 'Hmm?'

*Something puzzles them about the sombre way they have been thinking/
talking about rattlesnakes and screwing. They start to laugh –* **Alice**
with her breath, which is also a sound like crying.

Al Faaack! . . . Well, that's what they're there for – What!
Isn't it?

Alice Yes!

Al Breeding, isn't it?

Alice Like us, yes!

Al Like you – ! What – ! Three kids already – ! Isn't it – ?
Faaaaack! (*As elsewhere, 'Faaaaack' is a long, rasping, deep sound.*)

Alice But. (*She's moving into a new mood.*)

Al But you're right, yes, I will say this –

Alice No, but –

Al   That wire-mesh-and-timber dwelling's spotless clean.

Alice   Yes, it is, but –

Al   What?

Alice   No but, what's the complaint? This is a nice area, this is a new house, nice estate, neighbours, Marco Polo, too, – nice, old, just-a-bit-of-a-silly, old codger – What's the complaint? Do you see what I mean? Decent car!

Al   Great mortgage –

Alice   For next to nothing!

Al   'Cause Bill works in the bank.

Alice   And the children all healthy, thank God, thank God!

Al   So, you see!

Alice   Well off, up and down, wall-to-wall and off the wall.

Al   What is wrong with that?

Alice   What is wrong with that?

Al   Indeed! Look at her!

Alice   Spoilt.

Al   Look at her: happiness.

Alice   Some little thing, yeh know, back there.

Al   Some little thing, yeh know, back there *again* today, was upsetting her.

Alice   And it has passed.

Al   And it has passed, as like as not.

Alice   Yeh know? (*And she drinks. And thinks.*)

Al   And as is her custom for this holy half-hour, she is sitting quiet, here upstairs, in the attic room my dear, in the afternoon my dear, stocktaking her assets, mental and material, and not unmindful of her prospects?

Alice *nods.*

Al With the Famous Grouse whisky disguising her coffee, before collecting the children from school.

Alice And why not?

Al I ask you!

Alice And why not – should it enter my pretty head – a morning nip or two for elevenses as well?

Al Why not, indeed!

Alice Indeed, why not! It stops a person from smashing a – ! (*Sudden anger, the cup held out, as if she is going to let it fly.*)

A forward thrust of **Al**'s *head, encouragement to violence. But* **Alice** *contains herself.*

Alice Yes?

Al Thirteen seventeens?

Alice Two hundred and twenty-one.

Al Correct. Why do women have small feet?

Alice Chiphhh! (*Rejecting the question. She is looking around the room.*)

Al Chiphhh! And as attic rooms come, this one would hardly qualify as the brightest, would it?

Alice I like it this way.

Al Murky.

Alice Dusky.

Al Dusty, actually dirty.

Alice It's the only place in the house left untamed. Where else is there to sit?!

Al And you like a broken chair?

Alice   I do. And – well?! (*With a gesture at the floor.*) Is someone suggesting that downstairs with the radio is a serious alternative to up here?

Al (*her ear cocked to the floor*)   You have a point. Who's that singing?

Alice (*listening*)   That's what's-her-name. (*She sings, half-yodelling.*) She belongs up the Alps.

Al   Bit of a contest going on down there with the washing machine.

Alice *is making sounds that are meant to be the tune of the song on the radio – alternating from normal to falsetto, or high-pitched, nasal, Indian singing, perhaps;* **Al**, *in contest, is making sounds that imitate a washing machine.* (*Roles can be reversed.*)

Al (*interrupting the contest*)   Washing machine is winning!

Alice (*interrupting the contest*)   New pop star, what's her name?

Al   What is her name?

Alice   Anorexia Clunt.

Al   Faaaaack!

They are laughing. **Alice** *is about to become pensive again.*

Al   Ah no – ! Forget that – I know – ! Got it! (*A topic.*) Back to our old friend DJ. Speak to me about your husband, love.

Alice   My Bill?

Al   Your Bill, Big Bill, Solid Bill.

Alice   Well! He's good to the budgies. (**Al** *nods.*) He's good to me. (**Al** *nods.*) honesty is his bullet-proof vest. (**Al** *nodding.*) And soon he will manage a section.

Al   Strikes me – would I be right in speculating he is a man who likes a well-ironed shirt?

Alice   Absolutely. (**Al** *nods, wisely.*) He'll never look at another woman.

Al   You'll always know where he is.

Alice   My mother was right about him on that score.

Al   Yes, love?

Alice   And you could eat your dinner off the floor in the apiary out there. Oh, did you hear –

Al   Well, d'you know what I'm going to say to you?

Alice   No.

Al   It's hard to beat the Irish mother after all. Sure they always had the wisdom sure and the love that endures. But sorry, love, I interrupted you there.

Alice   Not at all – What was I going to say?

Al *and* **Alice**   Ahmm.

Al   A bright heifer with a clever tongue will be the last to sell at a market? (**Alice***: 'No'.*) For bedroom eyes look at their hairline? (**Alice***: 'No'.*) Your daddy looked at other women and he drank? (**Alice***: 'No'.*) It takes fourteen seconds, total, you reckon, to conceive three children, Bill's way?

Alice   No, stop that. What was I saying?

Al   Ah! That you could eat your dinner off the floor in the – (*And she points.*)

Alice   Yeah. Well, I kid you not, but did you hear that discussion this morning?

Al   Who?

Alice   On the radio: DJ, DJ, and a panel in discussion, did you?

Al   No. What was the subject?

Alice   Shit. I kid you not. And though he didn't actually use the word shit –

Al   He?!

Alice   Meant the word shit when he said he was told that, as against the *entire* animal kingdom, a bird will create more shit, pound for pound, ounce for ounce –

Al   And you could eat your dinner off the floor in the – (*She points.*) out there?

Alice   Pound for pound, ounce for?! Flabbergasting?

Al   Fucking rocks!

Alice   What is the first thing you think of –

Al   He said – ?

Alice   When you think of a place – coop or a yard – with a lot of chickens?

Al (*silently*)   Shit? (**Alice** *nods.*) None of the panellists beat you to the answer to that one?

Alice   Chicken shit.

Al   Yes, love?

Alice   Curiously, after the bird, the fish is next.

Al   Pound for pound, ounce, ounce – ? Wow!

Alice   That's why hatcheries, fish farms, densely populated dontcha know, are causing sea-lice on salmon.

Al   Never!

Alice   Wasn't I listening! The most heated discussion about anything in a long time.

Al   Speak to me more about fish shit, love.

Alice   And I wouldn't've minded, but Bill would've settled the matter, cleared it all up for them in a jiffy.

Al   Banker Bill.

Alice   Solid Bill.

Al   Wowee!

Alice *looks at her watch.*

Al   You'll go in a mo, plenty of time, you won't be late –
Have another.

Alice   He's very selfish. (*She gets the bottle and toys with it, or
just looks at it, blankly.*) Yes?

Al   And though Wowee Big Bill is doing well . . .

Alice   Yes.

Al   A degree course at night . . .

Alice   Yes.

Al   Breeding budgies and babies and suchlike, to boot . . .

Alice *nods.*

Al   And though he is the father of all three children, your
opinion, unbiased, objective?

Alice   He's not the sharpest knife in the drawer.

Al (*'but'*)   His honesty.

Alice   Oh, *his* honesty, uprightness, his blindness, his mental
deafness. Yeh know? His. His attributes may be matters of
wonder to his mother, as indeed they are to my mother, that
one time procurer, but I come in here somewhere too, do I
not? D'you know how boring it is, this, this, this drinking is?
D'you know how boring it is? . . . Boring . . . His *schoolbooks*!
His – his –

Al   Fucking – !

Alice   Moustache! The time he spends trimming it, looking
at it, sculpting it. His – his –

Al   Fucking – !

Alice   Fountain pens – ! Pencils! His –

Al   Fucking – !

Alice   Pink-striped shirt –

Al   Fucking – !

Alice   Hounds-tooth shirt – ! Matching –

Al   Fucking –

Alice   Coloured –

Al   Fucking –

Alice   Breast-pocket handkerchiefs!

Al   Well, he's a man!

Alice   No, this is serious. Or am I being selfish? I practically wipe his arse for him. My name is Alice – aged twenty-five – Who's Alice – ? *I'm* spoiled?

Al   Leave him.

Alice   Hah! Not feasible. (*She's dependent.*)

Al   Shoot yourself.

Alice   Yeah. I think about it. Drowning. We get into the car, drive to the docks and – (*Gestures 'drive over the edge'.*)

Al   With the children.

Alice   My beautiful children. Sandra, Karen-Marie, William. I couldn't leave them behind me . . . Aged six, five and four-and-a-half.

She begins to laugh – at the last, it would appear; it very quickly becomes harsh laughter, intense, a low-pitched rasp.

Al   Faaaack!

Alice   Faaaaak – !

Al   Faaaack – !

Alice   Faaaaaack – !

Al   Faaaaaack – !

Alice *and* **Al**   Faaaaaaaa . . . ck!

Which ends in tears, **Alice***'s. She puts away the bottle, this time without having poured anything from it.*

Al   And she used to be – very, they said – intelligent.

Alice   What am I to do?

Al   Look at her now, the creature.

Alice   I've no one to talk to.

Al   It's slob time. Your daddy, love.

Alice   If my daddy were alive.

Al   And he used a spare room, too.

Alice   Well, no garage, he used the spare room as a workshop for his metalwork.

Al   All kinds of tools in there.

Alice   *Two* steel vices, hacksaw, what's that?

Al   That is a caulking tool.

Alice (*and*)   That?

Al   Scribers.

Alice   Dividers, calipers, micrometer.

Al   And –

Alice   A magic magnet.

Al   And –

Alice   A ball-pein hammer, a rat-tail file –

Al   And a bottle hidden under the bench.

Alice   My mother drove him to it, my mother treated him like a dog.

Al   And you wished him dead.

Alice   No, *in*correct.

Al   Because he looked at other women and he drank. You wished him dead.

Alice   Well, I don't wish it now, okay?! Actually, I've started looking at other men. Actually, I'm going to have an affair.

Al   I wish you would – I'm bored to death – do *some*thing.

Alice   Well, if I had the time I would!

Al   Pathetic, pitiable and you know it. Thirty-nine eighteens? Oh?

'Oh?' in reaction to **Alice***'s quick movement getting the bottle again, to pour a generous measure into her cup.*

Alice   *'En voulez-vous encore, Madame?' 'Oui, un peu.' 'Mais non, Madame.' 'A mon grand regret, je me vois force de.'* Soupçon.

Al   Ay-yi! Ay-yi-yi – ! *Excrément* – ! *Mon Dieu* – ! *Merde* – ! *Calice!*

Alice   Thirty-nine eighteens, seven hundred and two, what is the difference between a duck, one of its legs is both the same, why does a mouse when he spins? (*And drinks.*)

Al   Because the higher the fewer.

Alice   Correct. Why do women have small feet?

Al   So that they can stand close to the sink.

Alice   Correct, correct.

Al   And time's up.

Alice   I'll be off now in a minute. (*Mellow, smiling throughout.*)

Al   You seem happy: is everything alright?

Alice   No but, really, d'you know what I think, do you? D'you know what I think? Law. Law is the only thing to do, is the only thing to take up, to study. Yeh know? I'd love to do Law, that's what I'd love. That's what I'm going to do. It's, yeh know, my dearest wish. (*She drinks.*)

A chirrup from outside.

Al (*absently*)   A budgie sings solo, Marco Polo twerps back a reply from his garden, the Dow Jones has plunged eighty-five points in panic trading. (*And she retires a little: perhaps to the upstage side of the mirror.*)

Alice (*as before, smiling throughout*)   I tell a lie. It isn't. Sandra
will do Law. The stage, *definitely, definitely*, for Karen-Marie.
And William? (*She laughs/smiles, fondly, at William's character.*)
My sweet William. But for me, it has to be, oh, yeh know?
What I want has to be, oh . . . (*She can't find the words but she
is inhaling an 'O', sucking in the air: and again.*) 'O' – (*Her free
hand moving in a wide gesture. She wants to breathe, space, room,
freedom to develop/discover her mind and spirit.*) Yeh know?
Because there's a strange, savage, beautiful and mysterious
country inside me. Otherwise, well, give me – a bucking
bronco – to deal with, because this is slow death. Or. Or.
Disfigure me. Mastectomy. Lobotomy. Abuse me, totally,
utterly, absolutely, ignore me. Let me have to depend on
others. What? *What?* To have to depend on others is the
worst suggestion I've heard today, I've ever heard. Chiphhh!
(*She sits there, smiling dreamily to herself.*) I'll be off now in . . .
just one sec more . . . to collect my fondlings, my beootiful
children. (*Then she looks at her watch.*) Christ! The children!
(*She's up and doing.*) Yes? Yes. (*And she puts away the bottle.*) Yes?
Car keys on the hall table, peppermints in the glove
compartment. Yes – ? (*About to leave.*) Big Al, am I heading
for trouble?

Al   Why are you asking the question? (*Which is the answer.*)

Alice   Okay. Am I going crazy?

Al   Bit of air getting in up there alright, I'd say.

Alice   Would I ever do anything silly?

Al   I don't know.

Alice   I wouldn't. I wouldn't ever even harm a fly.

From outside, the twittering of birds.

Al   I cannot think what it was was upsetting me, but it's
gone. Yes? Cup and saucer? (*Checks that they are in her hand.*)
Cup and saucer – correct. So! *Alles ist in Ordnung?* I'll leave
that one with you.

And she's gone. Swathe of light and combined sounds of radio and washing machine returning and disappearing again as from door opening and closing. Outside, the twittering is now grown loud and agitated, and comes in waves. **Al** *has continued there.*

Al   And outside, listen . . . for reasons best known or unknown to themselves, the budgies are singing all together like a hacksaw cutting through wire.

And fade.

By the Gasworks Wall

Characters

Alice
Jimmy
Bundler

Time: the nineties.

A lane. Dusk – almost night. It looks deserted. But is it? Because it's shadowy, badly lit.

Sounds off, not clearly defined, but they would appear to be those of a cattle mart in session, working late. (Words that have been spoken into a microphone, sound waves distorted, bent on the air coming over a distance.)

The rasp of a cough, off. Then, a shapeless kind of man of indeterminate age comes bundling along and, though he does not stop, as he disappears down the lane he does a full turn, to look back and into the shadows, as if suspicious of or sensing a presence there.

A moment or two later, off, the rasp of his voice again, this time as in meeting someone:

Bundler Goodnight!

And, a moment later, a woman comes along. She is preoccupied with herself, her head down, casually, carelessly dressed: top-coat hanging open, hands dug into the pockets and, perhaps, a head-scarf. And perhaps she has a slight limp. She's about forty.

As she disappears up the lane, a voice in a whisper from the shadows, calls:

Jimmy (*voice, off*) Alice!

She's disappeared from view. (A shadow moves?) The whisper is a little louder, more insistent this time.

Jimmy (*voice, off*) Alice!

Alice (*off*) Yes? . . . Yes?

Jimmy (*voice, off*) It's me!

Alice What? (*She is returning.*) . . . Who?

Jimmy (*voice, off*) Me! . . . Jimmy!

Alice . . . Jimmy?

Jimmy, *the 'Voice', has materialised slowly, as if nervous, unsure. Fully materialised, he is in his forties. The cut / length / style of his top-coat suggest expense / fashion / a bit of glamour. Headgear perhaps,* *spectacles perhaps – both as for a disguise. He has a rich baritone-type voice and when he laughs it, too, is rich.*

Jimmy James Godwin. Jimmy.

Alice . . . No.

Jimmy Yeah.

Alice I don't believe this.

Jimmy You can.

Alice I don't believe it, I do not believe it! Oh my God, my God, God! It is you. You look different.

Jimmy Well! (*Touches/removes headgear and spectacles – if he's wearing them – turns down the collar of his coat.*) And, no make-up.

Alice This is the absolutely most incredible thing that has happened to me in– I-don't-know-how-long – ever!

Jimmy You haven't changed.

Alice This is a surprise!

Jimmy You wrote.

Alice I know I did but I never for a second thought you'd – !

Jimmy Here I am!

Alice So what do I do with you now? (*She laughs.*)

Jimmy Why are you laughing?

Alice I mean, James Godwin, James Godwin!

Jimmy Jimmy, you always called me Jimmy. Actually, that was the only – dare one call it cautious – ? note in your otherwise very warm, I considered, very affectionate letter, I considered, your addressing me as James. Purpose in it?

Alice But everyone now knows you as James.

Jimmy So the formality of address was not a reserve of distance on your part?

Which she finds very funny, and he laughs too.

Alice   An awful lot of water under the bridge, Jimmy. It must be nearly twenty years since –

Jimmy   It's more. I was working it out on my way down. You were doing your leaving cert that year, you were all of seventeen – I came to work here end of '72, spring '73 we had our first date, which means –

Alice   We don't have to be too specific about the years.

Jimmy   It's twenty-one years ago. And twenty-one years since we last saw each other.

Alice   In the flesh.

Jimmy   What do you mean?

Alice   I see you often enough on the box.

Jimmy   Yes, a long time. Indeed.

Alice   And I haven't changed.

Jimmy   You haven't.

Alice   When I think of how I was back then! Tongue-tied!

Jimmy   No –

Alice   And I was a prude and I was stupid –

Jimmy   You were not! You were –

Alice   I was, I was – !

Jimmy   Quiet, maybe –

Alice   How did you put up with it?!

Jimmy   Unassuming, certainly –

Alice   Oh boy!

Jimmy   Not how I remember it, Alice.

Alice   Honestly! When things from my past come to mind now I feel so ashamed that I find myself talking out loud to myself – 'one, two, three, four' – to stop the embarrassment.

Jimmy   You were modest, you were shy, and you were right. You communicated inner beauty.

Alice   Well, compared with what young ones are said to be up to now, my attitude of then would qualify me today as an eighty-seven-year-old nun.

Jimmy   Actually, I was the one wasn't very communicative.

Alice   Oh you were –

Jimmy   Indeed, to a degree, I'm still like that. Because, I mean to say, communicating, I believe, has an element of hesitation about it? Is imbued with a fear? That in the process of communicating, one can be rejected? Would you agree with that observation?

Alice   Still the intellectual.

Jimmy   But-but-but, and then can follow, loss of self-esteem. You don't agree?

Alice   Oh my God! (*A reaction to a thought. Her lips lightly shut.*)

Jimmy   What, what?

Alice   One, two, three, four. The idea of a French kiss ('*back then*'). And how long were we going out together? Six, seven months?

Jimmy   A long time for a romance to last between young people – you see?!

Alice (*a beat, and*)   What are we talking about?!

They laugh.

Jimmy   You were perfect.

Alice   Thank you. Yeh know, I sometimes think I was. I'm very flattered ('*by all this*') . . . The last time I saw you was at the railway station. The railway was still operating then.

Jimmy   I still don't drive a car. People find that strange, hmm?

Alice   I don't. I don't drive any more. I haven't driven for, oh, over ten years. But that's another story. How did you get here?

Jimmy   Taxi.

Alice   A *taxi*?

Jimmy   I told him to wait.

Alice   I'm *doubly* very flattered . . . I don't know what to say to you!

Jimmy   You're doing fine! (*They are laughing.*)

Alice   I don't quite believe this yet!

Jimmy   Nor I, nor I! Why did you write to me?

Alice   Well!

Jimmy   But your timing?

Alice   I don't know. I don't know that we always know why we do things.

Jimmy   How true! That's very true.

Alice   Yeh know? (*She's flattered.*)

Jimmy   Interesting. (*He's hanging on her words.*) Yes?

Alice   I don't know that we always know. Write and ask him for a photograph, signed, I thought –

Jimmy   Yes – ?

Alice   Or is that childish, I thought –

Jimmy   Yes – ?

Alice   Then – a bit of a dream – ?

Jimmy   Or inspiration?

Alice   Or courage? Wouldn't it be grand to meet him?

Jimmy   I understand.

Alice   Yeh know? Maybe simply to explain why I was such an idiot at seventeen.

Jimmy   You were never that, Alice.

Alice   I remember! Or do I? When I was writing, I thought what if, instead of this waffle, what if I said something else: maybe, 'Dear James, it is high time we saw each other again to compare notes.'

Jimmy   Indeed. And you said as much.

Alice   I said as much?

Jimmy   'I imagine, that like myself, you have been through a great deal.'

Alice   I said that?

Jimmy   'And not all of it just success.'

Alice   Chiphhh!

Jimmy   'And it would be interesting to discover, first hand, where you're at now.'

Alice   Well! And I suggested we meet here?

Jimmy   You knew I'd know here: 'I'll be free to meet you in the Lane, any Tuesday, this October, seven o'clock!'

Alice   Well. I could have written: 'I'll be free to meet you, if you are free to do so, if you wish, any Tuesday, this October, in the hotel, seven o'clock.' Or 'Mocca Café, Shop Street, this October, seven o'clock!' It isn't as if by choosing here we are about to get up to anything, is it? Are we? We go for a coffee?

Jimmy   No. Your choice of venue appealed to me. We always came this way when we were making for the river. Sometimes we stopped here.

Alice   For mad passionate love.

Jimmy (*laughs, then*)   Everything would've happened at its proper time. Youngsters today are missing out. It's a shame.

Innocence has so much going for it. An energy unique to
itself. Excitement, exhilaration in the very balance of its own
waiting. Hmm?

Alice Anticipation?

Jimmy Alice. Quite, quite wonderful. It was an important
moment for me to receive your letter. Your letter was very
insightful.

Alice Well. Yeh know?

Jimmy And timely.

Alice Put it in an envelope, care of GTV, 'Please forward
if necessary', I suppose, into the postbox, quickly, I'm sure,
before I could change my mind?

Jimmy Yes?

Alice Well. I get these flashes of inspiration – Well, people
have told me that I do. Not often, of course, every couple of
years.

Jimmy Yes – ? Interesting – Like?

Alice I suppose, like . . . There's this book of poetry –

Jimmy Yes?

Alice My father gave it to me – Nice, yeh know – ?
Flowers from Many Gardens – and if I was a bit down I used to
dip into it one time and I'd find it – in spite of my
determined self to be otherwise – uplifting.

Jimmy Yes.

Alice Well, in this class, course, that I'm doing up town
there's this woman friend – well, acquaintance, really,
because as if the world wasn't bad enough she is one high-
maintenance type. Know what I mean? And I thought, is
that book of poetry still in the house somewhere? Found it,
gave it to her, 'Read this,' I said, 'and it will repay you a
thousandfold.'

Jimmy Yes, I've gone back to Spenser – Yes?

Alice   The power of some things – poetry, Jimmy, like, yeh know? I'm not saying that it wrought, wrought, a complete metamorphosis – hmm – ? in her, but she's now a *comparatively* disasters-free area. Yeh know? Yeh know? Another kind of – flash – I might get might be, oh, well, obviously, would be getting in touch with an old friend – 'High time!' Discover where *you're* at, 'first hand', and sensing that that getting in touch again might be somehow very important.

Jimmy   Were you here last Tuesday?

Alice   I passed here, same time. And I'd've been here next Tuesday, DV, and Tuesday week, seven o'clock.

Jimmy   I considered coming down last Tuesday, but . . .

Alice   You're busy.

Jimmy   No. Well, yes. I thought about it, but . . .

Alice   It's quite a trip to make.

Jimmy   You have children?

Alice   I have three.

Jimmy   I have three.

Alice   Nearly *touché* there. I didn't know if it was two or three you had. Though you do the news and you host those special things, you don't give much away about yourself?

Jimmy   You think that a bad thing?

Alice   Chiphhh! (*'No'.*) I can't wait to get rid of my three. Well, the two girls. I'm not particularly cut out to continue as their housekeeper. Whereas, my William, now: you cannot imagine what a gallant escort a little boy can be. And still is. Still, to have time to myself, to read, or – D'you know what I'd like to take up? Philosophy. I'd like to make sense of – well, myself for a start. Oh boy! Because . . . I'm talking too much.

Jimmy   Everything you say has a particular resonance for me. You were perfect. I shouldn't be harping on about it?

Alice Harp away.

Jimmy (*laughs; then, joking*) So, Tuesday is your evening off, then?

Alice Tuesday evening is for my creative writing class.

Jimmy Oh?!

Alice Thursday morning every fortnight: book club.

Jimmy Yes – yes?

Alice More opium for the housewife.

Jimmy Music – There was a choir in the town?

Alice Not particularly cut out to be a chorus girl.

Jimmy But surely – come along! – this writing class?

Alice Useless. If I hear another woman reading out a piece about remembering her daddy shaving when she was a girl, I'll shoot myself – with a razor.

Jimmy (*laughs*) I remember your father. A few times, walking in that direction, to Wood, he cycled past us, no acknowledgement?

Alice My mother's doing.

Jimmy Aaah!

Alice 'Get up on your bike outa that, Paddy Joe, and let them know I know where they are and if they're up to anything'. He died fourteenth of July, 1978.

Jimmy A young enough man then.

Alice Fifty-seven. She's still alive. He had a problem. (*A drink problem.*) Which, in family tradition, I upheld for a while, until I was brought to my senses with a bump.

Jimmy Oh?

Alice Car crash.

Jimmy A bad one?

Alice   Ahmm! We came out of it alive. My mother was keen on you.

Jimmy   She was?

Alice   Keen on you for me. She put a lot of store in anyone who worked in the bank. Look, neither of us, I think, are looking for kisses or that kind of thing, but – Or are we? (*She has taken his hand.*) But, just this, just for a minute.

They stand there holding hands, looking ahead at nothing, in their own thoughts, the night around them.

Alice (*smiles*)   Which of us is dreaming this? . . . So how're things? . . . Are you alright? . . . Are you well? Fed up?

Jimmy (*smiles, shakes his head; then*)   Will you be my man?

Alice *smiles, remembers: it's a game they used to play. She nods, 'Yes'.*

Jimmy   Will you carry the can?

Alice   Yes.

Jimmy   Will you fight the fairy?

Alice   Yes. Will you be afraid?

Jimmy   No. Phuh, phuh, phuh, phuh!

Alice (*overlapping*)   No. Phuh, phuh, phuh, phuh! . . . I suppose we wouldn't be here if things were alright . . . (*Then suddenly.*) You aren't researching something?

Jimmy   Researching? No. Why d'you ask?

Alice   No why. I just – (*With a shrug: 'wondered'.*) I walk a lot. The river occasionally, the wood, what's left of it. To get away. And away from *what*? Because if anything, there's increasingly nothing to get away from. D'you know that word 'estranged'? Well, why wouldn't you, you know words. So, things are getting emptier. So I'd say, 'What if I was that person?' (*Or.*) Her? No good. Okay. Well, 'What would it be like to meet that person?' Her, him, Jack-the-lad, film star, you, a ghost? . . . Yeh know?

Jimmy   Your husband.

Alice   Bill. He's fine, he's okay. Very good. He is good. We don't talk much. He would like me to have all sorts of things: a full-time housekeeper – (*Shakes her head, she wouldn't have it.*) No – To take up golf – No. I know why he offers those things. He arrived in town, oh, not too long after you'd left and, like you, to work in the National Bank, respectable position. Studious disposition. And it has stood him in good stead, as they say. He's done well for himself.

Jimmy   Has he?

Alice   Very well. We have a big house. It has a 'drive', in The Grove, my dear. Though, a funny streak has appeared (*'in him'*).

Jimmy   Yes?

Alice   Yeh know, for someone who never went out much, yeh know, socialised, and who didn't take his first drink until he was thirty-one. Well, in the last nearly two years he's, he's begun to knock it back.

Jimmy   Does he, you know, become – ?

Alice   No.

Jimmy   I mean violent.

Alice   No. But I've noticed something frankly ugly happening to the shape of his mouth. Yeh know? And I look at my own, in the mirror to check on it. And Murphy's pub – it was probably called something else in your time – down near the railway. Well, Murphy's is – what-would-you-call-it – ? the *roughest* pub in town. I've never been in it but I know the kind that goes in there and as clientele? Sub-human. I mean, he's area manager for half the banks in the country, for God's sake! So what is he doing, what is the matter with him?

Jimmy   Colleagues.

Alice   What?

Jimmy   Colleagues getting at him. Jealousy.

Alice (*silently?*)   What?

Jimmy   Oh-ho-ho!

Alice   *What* am I saying? This is not what I want to be talking to you about. Or remembering, when you're gone . . . It's not that I'm, yeh know . . . (*'unhappy'.*)

Jimmy   I know. Nor I.

Alice   Unhappy, I'm not saying that.

Jimmy   No.

Alice   Three children each.

He nods.

. . . By the same woman?

Jimmy   Yes.

Alice   What's she like?

Jimmy   She's very intelligent. She's no fool.

Alice   Like me. But there's something wrong, isn't there?

Jimmy   There is something missing.

Alice   I've never earned my living.

Jimmy   Something has been lost.

Alice   Yeh.

Jimmy   Yes.

Alice   . . . D'you remember an evening, actually it was night because I remember there was moonlight: we got to the river and you saw . . . Company.

'Company': someone is approaching. They draw back into the deeper shadows; **Jimmy** (*his back to us*) *standing facing* **Alice**.

Bundler *comes along and, without stopping:*

Goodnight!

Jimmy   Goodnight!

Bundler *is gone.*

Alice   He knows very well it's me here.

Jimmy   Who is he?

Alice   Nobody. He pretends to be a domesticated animal but he isn't. (*She's a good mimic of his rasping voice.*) 'Goodnight!' He's a known newsmonger, though. 'Jesus, d'ye know who I seen just now down the Lane in the dark with a stranger?' (*Good mimicry again.*)

Jimmy   Will he?

Alice   Who cares!

Jimmy   Do you want us to move?

Alice   No! (*Mimicry pitched townwards, defiance in it.*) 'Jesus, some fuckin' hurlers them Cork boyos!' My mind will dine on our meeting here for a long time.

Jimmy   You were going to say: 'An evening, night, we'd got to the river and I – ?'

Alice   . . . Must have been a lie, I can't remember. But I remember laughing.

Jimmy   Yes?

Alice   And at *what*? (*Laughing.*)

Jimmy   Yes? Yes? (*Laughing.*)

Alice   Your imagination.

Jimmy   My? Did I?! – Did I?!

Alice   Oh yes! Just letting your imagination rip –

Jimmy   Gobbledygook – ? Yes – ?

Alice   The things you came up with – ! Came out with – !

Jimmy   Did I?! – Yes?! – Did I?! – Did I?!

Alice   Oh yes! I can't remember what they were but, oh yes! And hearing myself laughing, you know?

Jimmy   Very interesting – !

Alice   I didn't have much to say for myself but –

Jimmy   You had a sense of the true personality –

Alice   But, yeh know, me listening to me, laughing – !

Jimmy   Inner self in celebratory response –

Alice   'Can this be *me* making this sound?'

Jimmy   Considering your normal reserved nature?

Alice (*laughing*)   What? No! Yes! I don't know!

Jimmy   Spontaneity of the thing – Wonderful! Purity of the thing. Oh, yes.

A beat or two and **Alice** *laughs out again, to herself.*

Jimmy   You don't agree?

Alice   I do, oh, I do!

Jimmy (*musing*)   Oh yes . . . Yes, and artists now for instance – I don't know if you would agree with this – are another example – Actors. I've a lot of actor friends and, you know, they are invariably shy. (*Laughs.*) The good ones, that is, we're not talking – cravats here? Though, indeed, mind you, I went around wearing one myself one time. (*And he's deadly serious again.*) But-but-but, the shyness factor, humility, is to be found only in the consummate artist, the one who, somehow, in his work manifests, exposes, the deepest inner self. You agree? For all the shyness, humility! You don't agree?

Alice   I do.

Jimmy   You agree?

Alice   Yeah.

Jimmy   Yes, an enormous subject. Oh, yes . . . You were perfect, you know.

Alice   Well . . .

Jimmy   What?

Alice   Maybe.

Jimmy   And I was so . . . (*Probably 'stupid'. He shakes his head.*) I've made a lot of mistakes in my time. Life is a game of bad shots, Alice. What?

Alice   Par for the course. What really decided you to . . . ? (*'Come down here.' She has realised that all is not well; and how is she to deal with the situation?*)

Jimmy   Decided me to? Yes?

Alice   Can't remember.

Jimmy   Sorry?

Alice   Scatty. Galloping Alzheimers.

Jimmy   What? (*Then laughs.*) Oh yes! Same as myself! Yes! The mistakes! Sometimes I think I'm going crazy – What?!

Alice   I don't think, I'm *going* crazy, I think I *am* crazy! (*She laughs, inviting him to laugh.*) I've all the evidence of it, d'you know what I mean? Then – confusion – I go up town, into the supermarket, I see people – people I have known from childhood – the strangest faces on them, obscenely feeling up the vegetables – for crying out loud! – for crying out loud! – neighbours, my neighbours' determination to get the daisies – for crying out loud! – to kill every last poor daisy on their lawns – and, after all that's happened, – scandals, scandals! – they're still running up and down to the church praying – to who, to what? D'you know what I mean, Jimmy? I'm *confused*. They are the *normal* people? Makes me think, makes me wonder if, after all, sanity isn't just another form of insanity. D'you know what I'm saying, Jimmy?

Jimmy   Yes. Suicide.

Alice   How d'you mean?

Jimmy   As a subject.

Alice   Oh, suicide, I see.

Jimmy Yes?

Alice How many times have I thought of it, how many times!

Jimmy I've been thinking about it a good deal lately. You know?

Alice How many times have I thought of it, I ask you!

Jimmy That, or make a new start.

Alice How d'you mean?

Jimmy You know, to start again. You know? I think I know your husband without ever having met him. You know? I think I know him. He's done very well for himself? So have I. Money? Extraordinary! He's a very senior figure. He has to see that standards are maintained, he has to remind others that codes of behaviour have to be upheld. So what happens? Jealous and resentful colleagues – both genders. Subtle harrassment. Vicious and malicious whisperers. He's become a difficult man. Why wouldn't he?! He's become violent – No! You denied it too quickly when I asked you earlier. Oh-ho-ho! He's a violent man. And the shape of his mouth. I know him. I wouldn't mind finding a rough pub, if I could find the right one, to, to relieve the – if I considered that it would help – to, to relieve the, relieve the pressure – Right? – if I could find the right one, if I was fit enough for the right one, if I considered that that would be the answer.

Alice Hold on –

Jimmy You know, something to send one drunkenly, wonderfully, reeling home, you know, instead of – phhhhh! Pressure.

Alice Hold on a sec.

Jimmy Or something, yes, right, Alice, to sober one up to consider the alternative: to start again.

Alice But that isn't possible.

Jimmy   It's not possible for you to be seventeen again, for me to be twenty-three. But it's possible – it *is* possible – to backtrack to see if those emotions that were authentic then can be rediscovered. I've already started. Otherwise, what? Suicide? That's too much. But how much is it to continue to live out one's life accepting a world that is shallow, cynical, a painted thing? Should one not stop oneself subscribing to – evil? You mentioned the word shame earlier. I couldn't agree more. You know, I think everything I've done was a mistake. I ask how has this come about, this me, this talking sin, walking lie. No authenticity. The purity of what we shared back then by comparison, the cleanness of this interlude – short as it is – here this evening.

Alice   I don't know –

Jimmy   You, you were going to – Alice – ! You were going to say back there: a clear sky, a night sky, moonlight, you and I together by the river and that I saw something. Well, you're right. I think I did: see something. I'm not talking apparitions or any of that kind of nonsense. I *felt* it. You know.

Alice   Jimmy –

Jimmy   Please. Please. (*'Allow me to finish'.*) One simply cannot continue going through these periods of shame and guilt –

Alice   I don't feel –

Jimmy   Please. Please. Allow me to finish. These periods of shame and guilt. Recrimination: rows with onself, with others, merited, but in one's own mind. Anger: discovering that one's friends are only fair-weather friends, false friends, who – in my case – express admiration for me and for my work but who really hold me cheap and want to see my humiliation.

Alice   Your family.

Jimmy (*a simple brush of his hand deals with that subject*)
Colleagues, from the tea-boy up – vanity! – preening
themselves in the idea of celebrity gone mad, rampant. And
I'm concerned with objectivity, with standards – in the
newsroom for instance. I have spoken out: 'Are you reading
the news or do you consider that you are making it?' I want
nothing more to do with the world I've been working in.
I've already started – I told you – in a new direction, a path
of inner exploration that will – hopefully! hopefully! – take
me back to the authenticity that is you, and that you
allowed me to share. Please. (*Allow him to finish.*) You said you
thought that contacting me might be important. Well – !
Please. You said – exact words – 'you sensed that getting in
touch again might be somehow *very* important.' Need it be
said how very important it is to me too? Perfect.

Alice   Where's the taxi, Jimmy?

Jimmy   The Square. I told the driver to have a meal in
the hotel.

Alice   I'll come up with you to the taxi.

Jimmy   No. We'll keep this to ourselves for the moment.
I'll go back, but I'll meet you here – tomorrow night? –
would that be okay? – same time, and we'll take it from
there, right?

Alice   Stay the night.

Jimmy   Stay?

Alice   In the hotel. I'd like you to meet a friend of mine.
He has a great manner, he's very bright and –

Jimmy   No. Keep this perfectly secret until we go further
into our discussion. Yeah. I'll go back – It will be midnight
by the time I get there. All sorts of things to begin seeing to
and wrap up. Yeah. Yeah.

Alice   Jimmy.

Jimmy (*again, to himself*)   Yeah.

Alice   Jimmy.

Jimmy   Alice.

Alice   I'm out there with you on – a number of things, but what I am, a lot of the time, is doing the ironing, and I'm bored. What I do a lot of the time is wonder was I seriously incapable of doing no more than producing three children. Maybe the reason I've continued dreaming in my near dotage is to stop me thinking of how much time I've wasted.

Jimmy (*'you are'*)   Perfection.

Alice   No, I'm not perfect or authentic. Never was, nobody ever was. I don't believe I'm saying this, but maybe it's time I said it – *to myself* – and got my head down from up there. Jimmy, Jimmy, listen to me! How do I put this? I'm a stupid housewife, growing stupider by the day by three stupid children, and I have an extremely stupid husband. Is this making any sense to you?

Jimmy (*'you are'*)   Not stupid.

Alice   Jimmy! Jimmy! You aren't well.

Jimmy   No.

Alice   Meat factory, cattle mart, old gasworks behind that wall, Blackberry Lane. No blackberries but this Lane that we are standing on is a sort of short cut from my house to the town, and vice versa, obviously, and, obviously, I use it quite a lot to go to the town and return from the town to my house, to and fro, to and fro, and I was on my way – twenty-whatever minutes ago – to a poxy Tuesday night dynamic creative writing class – 'Pack your every word with TNT'. I think that same poxy creative writing might have contributed to my writing that letter. Homework is encouraged. Other than what you told me it contained, I really can't remember how I put it, how dynamically I phrased it, but I'm sure I didn't think you'd ever get to read it: some secretary or other would. Let alone your showing up here! We walk up to the Square? (*He doesn't move.*) 'Let's pretend we're kings and queens' is the scatty stupid side of me. I've wondered, for a long time, will this fantasising ever end, or, will a fantasy ever come true? Both have happened tonight. All I want from here on in – I promise – is reality. We go?

Jimmy   You promise.

Alice   Yes. Hmm? (*Meaning 'We go?'*)

Jimmy   That's excellent.

Alice (*a silent*)   Hmm?

Jimmy   You have finished playing games with yourself then . . . And with me?

Alice   No.

Jimmy   That's how you regard me?

Alice   Let's go.

Jimmy   May I ask you a question? . . . 'May I ask you a question' is too much to ask after I have gone to all this trouble to come down here and see you?

Alice   No.

Jimmy   Are you enjoying your triumph?

Alice   What tri –

Jimmy   Would you like the pictures?

Alice   I don't follow.

Jimmy   Photographic evidence . . . How much – to what degree – do you enjoy belittling me?

Alice   Not at all. I would never think of –

Jimmy   'Not at all I would never.' And I am to tamely accept humiliation?

Alice   Let's go, Jimmy.

Jimmy   Without retaliation?

Alice   I'm sorry if I've hurt you.

Jimmy If? Do you realise, because of your 'fantasising', that I could hurt you now. I could? I could?

Alice You could.

Jimmy And I would like to. Would that 'reality' suit you? Fear of consequences are not stopping me. I could kill you right now? I could?

Alice You could, Jimmy, but you won't.

After a moment he walks off. She inhales silently, deeply, and holds it. She is shaken. She reacts to someone approaching.

The cavalry.

She retires to the deeper shadows – it's just a step – to take another deep breath, to compose herself. **Bundler** *arrives with a man. (The man can be* **Alice***'s husband without making any issue whatsoever of it.) Their eyes are a little 'ungoverned' searching the place.* **Alice** *emerges from the shadows. They look at her, she regards them, coolly. Then as she walks off, leaving them there, passing them by, she winks to herself and in rasping imitation of* **Bundler***:*

Jesus, some game that, last Sunday! Goodnight.

At the Airport

Characters

Alice
Bill
Waitress
Waiter
Official

Time: 2005.

In the darkness and as the lights come up:

Alice (*voice-over*)   Has something happened? Did something happen? What am I doing here, what kind of place is here? What's happening?

*A **Waitress** is putting two plates of food on a table. That done, she will go to her station, to wait there, poised, tray clapped under her arm, for anybody's bidding.*

*A **Waiter** (upstage) is ushering a couple to the table. He seems a jolly sort – and would become jollier given the chance. He's elderly, perhaps old-world. He wears a dickey bow.*

Waiter   Down here alright, sir, madam? Alright? Alright?

*The sober-looking couple are **Bill** and **Alice**. **Bill** is pushing sixty, **Alice** is somewhat younger. They do not indulge the **Waiter**, they nod in acknowledgement of him without looking at him.*

Alice (*voice-over*)   What is that hissing noise? Sibilance. Like burning grass. And (*is that meant to be*) . . . music?

Waiter   Madam? (*Drawing back a chair for her.*)

Alice (*voice-over*)   Piped music. And idiotic pop songs and love songs and arias to promote – coition – (*She laughs four hollow, humourless syllables.*) – encourage the nonsense of it all to continue.

Waiter   Sir? (*Seating **Bill**.*)

Alice (*voice-over*)   Perpetuate the idiocy, the mistake, the human race.

Waiter   Alright now, alright, everything alright?

Alice (*voice-over*)   Humanity on a journey to nowhere.

Bill   And two glasses of water.

Waiter (*moving away*)   And two glasses of –

Alice (*voice-over*)   Has something happened?

The above is a kind of prelude to the play proper.

As **Waiter** *moves away – leisurely movement of feet throughout – a backward jerk of his thumb at the table and the accompanying mime of the other hand drinking from a glass: an order to* **Waitress**. *And he goes off* (*to deal with other diners*).

And **Waitress** *has gone into action, at once, going off to fulfil the order. Rather fast movement of feet throughout.*

A buzz of sound, a sibilance (*like that of burning grass*), *hangs over the place, mingling with what-would-seem-to-be faint, nondescript music. And perhaps, perhaps, there is some kind of an unreal – or chic – lighting affect.* (*Could be, maybe, a revolving light, coming from outside, washing the interior light.*)

In any case it's a bit strange. And we see only one table. The strangeness (*stylisation*) *can be put down to the idea that we are encountering this place through* **Alice**'s *odd mental state.*

Bill *is eating and continues, almost throughout, with his head down, movements of the cutlery precise. There are a couple of occasions when he glances at her, when he considers she will be unnoticing of it. She, now, is like someone suspended in a forgotten purpose* (*of, for example, unwrapping her knife and fork from the coloured paper napkin*).

Alice   Looking at it rationally the worst has happened. Has it? The worst? And it is conceivable that her heart is breaking. But is it? Because if it is, it is bearable. More's the pity. More's the pity that it is not what is believed to be the standard reaction to a breaking heart. Preferable that it should get on with it, break, conclude its business, that she should hear some kind of crack, perhaps, then the rush of chill air in through the crack, perhaps, that would bring numbness. Yes. Or that some kind of cloud, darkness, should descend to take care of everything. But that is unlikely, that is all nonsense, this is the way it is, this is how it goes, goes, continues, dully aching, no cure for it, slow, tedious, grey and yes, of course, bearable.

Waitress *arrives, tray clapped under her arm, to put two glasses of water on the table, to make a little bow as she backs away, and returns, silently, rather swiftly, to her station to await next orders.*

Neither **Alice** *nor* **Bill** *look at her, though each nods, in an automatic way, an acknowledgement of the service.*

Alice   Looking at it rationally the worst has happened, has it, and really, what is there to say about it? Not much. That woman over there looks familiar. Didn't she used to one time have a shop in – ? Not at all, that's crazy. The woman that used to one time own the paper shop in Shop Street would, if she were still alive, be a hundred years old now. (*Sudden, very minor agitation.*) What's happening, where am I?

Bill   Hmm? (*He's eager to be of assistance.*)

Alice (*still in her train of thought*)   Why am I here, what am I doing here?

Bill   Alice?

Alice (*to him*)   No. (*Meaning 'Everything's okay'.*)

Bill   I'm sorry?

Alice   Fine. (*And she busies herself for a moment or two unravelling the cutlery from the red paper napkin.*) Coloured tables, coloured chairs, coloured tiles on the floor, what kind of place is this? Why not balloons too? So many colours, yet colourless, elevated out of the ground floor on steel columns, accessed by an escalator. And that buzz of voices that hangs there, ascended from below, hanging in the air, strangely even, like dust caught in a haze of light, and pitiable music, continuous. A pall in sound, stopping only for – (*Buzz of sound has stopped.*) As if mankind down there holds its breath for – good news?

An announcement for an airline flight over a tannoy system. (The sound is recognisable rather than the message being distinguishable.)

Alice   Good news, no, so, mankind observes another moment's silence, this time out of pity for itself . . . (*Buzz of sound resumes.*) before remembering to start up again, the same as before, a daze in the head. What kind of place? A place as from a nightmare that is pretending to be a dream, where a party, or indeed a wake, will never really begin.

She has a sip of water, dabs her lips with the napkin and watches her husband eat.

She looks across the table at her husband who is eating a –
Who looks across the table? She looks across the table.
Who? She-she-her-she, this woman, me, looks across the
table at that man, her husband, who is eating a meal of fish
and chips in the manner of someone performing a duty and
who is he, she wonders. She knows that he's very rich, and
so is she, by association. So much money they don't know
what to do. She knows that his name is Bill. She knows too
that he does not want or need food right now, but a thing
once started will be completed, becomes a duty, a must that
has to reach done. Possibly admirable, who knows, who
cares? But that is how that man her husband is. And as he
will finish that meal in front of him, he will, in that
occupational way of his of finishing things, go on finishing
other things. Well, good luck to him if that's how he keeps
the world at bay, or keeps it happy, or tries, which possibly
makes it admirable too, enviable too, who knows, who cares,
possibly yes. But he sees himself as some kind of stoic. Men,
a lot of them, are like that. Whereas, emotionality, they
believe, would you believe in this post-post-feminist day and
age, emotionality is women's territory. Women weep – yes,
and they sometimes wail, howl, moan, shriek, squawk,
screech! – when a thing falls out, goes wrong, and thereby
somehow in the process, men believe, women cure themselves.
No such luck for men. It would make a person smile,
almost. It would nearly make a person cry.

During the above, **Waitress** *has again launched herself into motion in
response to somebody requiring her services. She has now returned and
awaits the next call.*

Alice   Really, there is no point in pushing an oblong of fish
around a plate in a pretence at an agreement of cutlery in
action on both sides of the table, or indeed in trying to
conceal from anyone that untouched food. He notices, of
course, and he dislikes waste, but, this evening, he will have
to put up with it. And he will put up with it because he is

not a bad man, and in view of what has happened, of
course.

She is looking in a new direction.

Party of young men. In transit from somewhere. What ages
are they? Yes. And the youngest? Yes. So pale. Young men
coming from a weekend-long spree, now feeling the exhaustion
of it, wanting to be home.

Waiter *appears, briefly – before ambling off again in another direction
– to gesture, with backward pointing thumb, to* **Waitress** *to attend a
table (the party of young men). And she is into motion, tray clapped
under her arm, order-pad at the ready, pencil (on a string), off to take
an order.*

Alice   Little more than boys. They look sluggish, their dress
awry. They must be baking in those heavy jackets in here.
The only item awry in the formal black and white (or 'the
formal dress') of the waitress are the brown stockings. An
immigrant? No.

Waitress *enters and exits to make good an order.* **Waiter** *enters, as
from somebody else's table, grinning, his jaw askew, and he goes off to
somebody's table. He is doing his rounds.*

Alice   He ambles because he is in charge. The dickey bow
must prove something. 'Alright, alright, everything alright?'
Every diner's friend, and becomes over-familiar, if allowed.
Everything's alright. (*And she laughs: four syllables, dry, hollow
humourless.*)

A sip of water. **Waiter** *has entered and is at the table. He is
grinning, his jaw askew.*

Waiter   Alright, alright, everything alright?

Alice *laughs her dry, humourless, hollow, four syllables.* **Bill** *lifts his
head but he does not look at* **Waiter**.

Waiter   Sir?

Bill   Yes. (*And, just as abruptly, has resumed eating.*)

Waiter   Alright? Madam?

Alice   Thank you.

Another suspension in the buzz of sound for another annoucement over the tannoy system, while **Waiter** *moves off, continuing his rounds; while* **Waitress** *comes in to deliver a tray of food to the young men's table, off. (She will return in some moments, tray clapped under arm, to go off for supplements.) While* **Alice** *has been continuing.*

Alice   He has been very good to her over the past nearly two days, in a formal manner, of course. Not that being informally good to her would have been better, would it? No, not really. On the contrary, not at all. He had supported her arm, well, touched her elbow, getting in and out of taxis, and again, though really it was unnecessary, at the hospital mortuary. The looks they had exchanged were few, accidents, they would hardly qualify as glances: as if he feared that she, she, this woman would swamp him if he gave her the opportunity, was it? *(She laughs her hollow laugh, four syllables.)* Tears? No. Twenty years ago, maybe – twenty-five, maybe, but not now, not any more, and a good thing too. Life now is grooved. Life is inescapably harsh, cruel, self-centred, ugly, sordid, mean. Tediously suffocating, stubbornly bearable. And humankind is vile. Well, think of it, people killing seals with – nails?

She is looking in the young men's direction again. **Waitress** *is taking a tray of things – supplements – to the young men. She will return in a little while to stand at her station, to leave again in a little while at someone's request.*

Alice   They have come awake, just about. Hunger. Young people. *(A sip of water.)* And there was a time when she used to think of life as serene. Or is she dreaming things now? *('And there was a time'.)* When her life was seventh heaven, 'soul-uplifting', things like that, capable of moments of self-forgetting bliss, things like that, rapture. Moments when it all made sense. A time, twenty-five, no, thirty years ago when everything seemed possible. And *was* possible? . . . Dreaming. She was a great dreamer. Back then she was a fool to any kind of suggestion: suggestion did not take no for an answer. 'It's no use trying,' said Alice, 'one cannot believe in impossible things.' 'You haven't been practising,' said the White Queen. (*Her husband again.*) He cares for her, in a civilised way. There was an ugly period about ten years ago, but he is more civilised now, and maybe so is she. To him, their relationship is a duty. Or is she and has she been getting it wrong? To her, it is a what? At the moment a not very good habit. For quite some time a silence has been growing between them, a distance, oh (for) one thing and another, this reason and that. She likes him. She never disliked him. And she concedes that she has contributed to the state of affairs. She can no more change her personality than he can his. And she has come to admire him. He didn't make excuses. He didn't let anything get in his way. And how many times has she felt it was unfair that he had not been dealt a hand, so to speak, better than hers? But she does not concede, agree to, accept the charge of her second daughter, the knowing, the learned, Karen-Marie, barrister-at-law, that she, the mother, has driven them all demented – 'bonkers' – to the extent that Sandra, the eldest, had to get out and has now disappeared-off with New Age travellers to spread shit, 'literally shit', all over the world – fine legalese – because that's all New Age travellers are good for. That she, Karen-Marie, barrister-at-law and neurotic, never wants to see or speak to her mother again, that the youngest, William – 'Your darling, your pet' – will soon, if he does not already do so, feel the same way about her and be off to join the circus to get away from her. 'And!' before resting her case and taking it up again, before leaving and slamming the front door behind her, 'You-are-treating-my-father-like-a-dog.' (*Her dry, hollow four-syllable laugh. Then:*) The defendant begs to differ. Children are not meant to lie nesting for ever, and late, in the family home. Whate'er befalls them when they do leave is not at issue here. And with reference to canines and their treatment – thereof, if anybody wishes – may it further please the court to know, as testament to the defendant's good character in the matter, that it was she who took in the strays, and that it was she and she alone who looked after them, and that the succession of Snout, Snap and Marilyn was regarded by all who knew them as a line that had well and truly fallen on its paws. (*The young men's direction again.*) They have broken something: fair-headed, littlest one has – a glass, knocked it over and broken it while trying to remove his anorak without standing up. The others hardly notice.

Bill   Would you like something else?

Alice (*overlapping*)   The dickey bow has. He (*Bill*) has said something. (*To him.*) Hmm?

Bill   Would you like something else?

Alice   Ahmm.

Bill   We don't know how much longer we'll be here.

Alice   Yes.

Bill   A glass of wine?

Alice   Yes! What did he say?

Bill   Waiter!

Alice   Glass of wine, yes of course, glass of wine, yes: the thought was a practical one, something to be doing, occupying, under the circumstances and, true, they do not know how much longer they shall have to wait. He is a very private man. Well, he isn't able to be anything else, is he? He knows it. But his guard occassionally slips. He's bad in company. That morning, New Year's morning party at their neighbour's, astonishing to hear him – you could hear him all over the room – declare, in challenging tones, that his greatest distaste in life was for lame people. Lame people. What did he mean? That they were an affront to his own firm step. He must have read it somewhere. And, likely as not, misinterpreted it. Then went on to exceed himself – he couldn't stop himself – declaring, in challenging tones his other great distastes for the human imperfections in others. Shyness and self-consciousness in company drove him to that kind of thing, yes, but that he believed in his offensive remarks was true also.

Waiter (*arriving*)   Alright, alright, everything alright?! (*He is grinning, jaw askew, and he's holding out his hand, which contains the shards of a broken glass.*) What?! What?!

Bill   Two glasses of red wine.

Waiter   What?! What?! They're still rearing them, what?!

Bill   Your house wine will be fine. (*And he's already resumed eating or sipping from his glass of water.*)

Waiter (*to himself*)   Still rearing them.

Alice   He's offended.

Waiter   Stella!

Alice   I think he has drink taken.

Waitress, *from somewhere, to his side to take the broken glass from him, the order 'Two glasses of red,' the signal to her feet – a nod of her head – and she's gone again.* **Waiter** *continues there, absently, for a moment, wondering which is the best way to go for company. The usual break in the buzz of sound for another annoucement is happening.*

Alice   That distorted jaw.

Waiter (*moving off*)   Still rearing them.

Alice (*the* **Waiter**'s *jaw*)   In another it would be a tooth problem, in him it's something cranky, for all his attempts to be a comedian. (*Then:*) 'Still rearing them.' (*And her hollow, dry four-syllable laugh.*) The last time she and her husband had a glass of wine together was the night before their son left home. William. She had made a fish pie because that was the dish her son liked best. Not quite a party: still – and considering the usual quietness of the house and the usual very private nature of the father – his remarks about Polonius were nice, pleasant – and considering the undemonstrative type that the mother had become – it was an occasion. An occasion. Three people had made an effort, and they had been successful in that effort. And she hopes this minute, if it's happening this minute, that they are handling the coffin gently off the plane. If that matters, of course. Does it matter? Perhaps it does. Perhaps not, really. No.

Waitress *is arriving, two glasses of wine in her hands, tray clapped under her arm; she has to bend her knees to put the wine on the table; in the bent-kneed position, for a brief moment she holds a look on* **Alice***; then she bows as she backs away and returns to stand and wait at her station.*

Alice (*as* **Waitress** *arrives*)   Why have a tray if one is to carry glasses in one's hands? (*She nods her acknowledgement of the service, as does* **Bill**.) That look: a woman frightened of her own timidity, is it, concern for an untouched plate of fish and chips, is it? A creature that would prefer to run rather than walk, is it? Look, look, look, who's interested? So, William is dead, and so, too, her mother, last October. And she was sad at her mother's 'passing' and sad, too, that her mother was not the clever woman that she thought she was. Her espousing causes was ridiculous, contradictions of herself. Feminism? She was a man's woman, she fawned on them, with, of course, the exception of her own husband. He died fourteenth of July, '78, twenty-seven years earlier. At least he had a sense of humour. 'Classical music and your mother, Alice? Putting on airs?' 'Feminists?' Loudly. 'The lash across their backs for them and the harem.' But in drink, without saying a word, he could fix you with his eyes as if he were pinning an insect to a board, as if you were the hated enemy. There was a moment, though, when they were about to place the lid on the coffin and she had this urge, to rush to them, stay them for a moment, to look at him for a last time and say – something. Goodbye. She did no such thing of course. She often wished him dead. (*She has a sip of wine and:*) Tepid, dull, cheap-dry, the life taken out of it. (*And smiles.*) Drinkable: bearable. They talk about the unnatural event of a child predeceasing parents, but what about the crops of children, crops of young men sent off to war and never come back? Millions. Millions of them – and smiling. That begins to put things in perspective now, doesn't it? He slipped, simple as that. Leaning up against a wall, eating a bag of chips, his feet slipped out in front of him from under him, his head hit the footpath. She did not – really and truly – want further details. It wasn't as if he had been – kicked? Simple accident, plenty of witnessses, including that young girl who was with him at the time. She has the medical report in her handbag, which she can look at, sometime, if she wishes to. There is the police report too, delivered into their hands by a policeman, its contents explained in considered – and considerate, she could see – language. 'Just in case,' the policeman said. Just in case of what? They wanted to sue the footpath? A priest attended because they were Irish, to offer comfort, and he did his best. It was God's will. God chose your William. Now, to the woman sitting here, if God is anything at all he is Godlike. He, She, It cannot be explained in terms of being choosy. God is the name given to the unknown. The unknown is possibly – and probably – nothing. It's not a great line in theology to say that God, the unknown, wills, picks, chooses this or that, no more than it is sensible to suggest that he can spend his time counting the hairs on your head, unless, that is, of course, he is otherwise engaged in being an all-seeing disgusting Peeping Tom. Unless, of course, he *does* will, pick and choose his targets, from William to earthquakes to the cat crossing the road, tsunamis and car crashes, in which case he is the Almighty Terrorist. There is no explanation for what cannot be explained, no comfort for what cannot be comforted. Useless to the dead and makes not the slightest difference to the bearable ache of the living. But she accepted the explanations and the religious platitudes for the sake of the people who offered them. Perhaps she should have asked the girl who was with him at the time for a few details, for the girl's sake – had they been to the cinema? – token elaboration, just to help the girl because she was young and the fright of the accident was still in her eyes. Oh, well!

Bill   Alice? (*He's smiling.*)

Alice   But, really, what she wanted to say to them all was –

Bill (*he wants to engage her, divert her/divert himself*)   I was looking, at *The Times* on our flight home and things in the US are very much on the up and up . . . Alice?

Alice (*to him*)   Yes?

Bill   So how is that for you under a Republican Administration and your most favourite president ever?

Alice (*to him*)   Hmm! (*Then:*) What did she want to say to them all?

Bill   And bully for Bush! And it would seem that the recovery is durable, self-enforcing, and job-creation is increasing – Yeah?

Alice   Yes.

Bill   There was that slowdown in the labour market from May onwards, last year.

Alice *nods.*

Bill   But that now has changed and as a sign of all this –

Alice   Yes –

Bill   The Fed has decided that it no longer needs to maintain interest rates at the abnormally low level they were at until recently.

Alice   *Oh*, yes.

Bill   Dollar continues to fall – let it fall –

Alice   What she wanted to tell them all was –

Bill   That's how they like it.

Alice   – that things occur, not because a divine power wills them –

Bill (*gives up*)   Theirs is a closed economy.

Alice   – or because any principle ordains them, but simply because that is the way things occur, they just happen. Things, accidents, happen for no particluar reason; for no purpose. Why go on with the rigmarolling? If people want to fill in their time by saying that there are conditions, causes or superstitious reasons for what happens to human beings, then let them have the courtesy to apply the self-same conditions, causes and superstitions for what befalls plants,

animals and – why not? – stones. This continual emphasis
that is put on the great importance of human life above all
else is a nonsense, it's pathetic. The sun – the sun! Galileo:
that-thing-book about him in the library! The sun does not
shine for humankind no more than it revolves round the
earth like they wanted it to one time. Pitiful. If humankind is
special it's because no other species on earth can rival
human viciousness.

Waitress, *who has been standing at her station for some time, is off
again to supply service to some quarter.* **Alice** *is taking a sip of wine
and is now looking in the direction of the young men's table.*

Alice   They are so pale. And wasn't there a time . . . well,
as far as one can remember these things . . . when she felt
that inside her there was something mysterious that she
thought of as herself. As far as she could make out there
was something special about her. Felt it, not thought it. And
though it gave her a sense of isolation, also, she trusted it.
All would come well. She too, would you believe, was the
world. What she was giving herself to had a purpose – it
could, would, overcome anything that opposed it – an end
that, when it came about, she would – understand? No.
Recognise. Recognise as the mysterious, beautiful and, yes,
savage reality of being alive. Sharing humanity . . . Well!
(*And she laughs her hollow laugh.*) It is conceivable that the worst
has happened and the reality of it leaves a lot to be desired.

Bill   Should I check on things downstairs?

She continues to laugh. He is toying with the wine glass.

Bill   Alice? Alice?

Alice   Oh! (*And raises her glass.*) Cheers!

Bill   Ah, no.

Alice   Hmm?

Bill   I'll check with Information downstairs and see how
matters are progressing.

Alice   Oh, yes.

Bill *goes off.*

Alice   He's checking on what-did-he-say? Did she say 'Cheers!'? She couldn't have said 'Cheers', could she? Why would she say that? *('Look'.)* Does it matter? Perhaps it was that she'd been feeling the stem of the glass like this and – does-it-matter? It doesn't matter. He said he was going downstairs to check on matters downstairs.

Waiter *(arriving)*   Alright, alright, everything alright? Finished, finished, we clear away, Madam?

Alice   Thank you. Leave the wine.

Waiter   Stella!

The last to **Waitress** *as he moves off, backward jerk of his thumb and suitable gesture/mime with the other hand for* **Waitress** *to clear the table.* **Waitress**, *at that moment, is en route to deliver a tray of things to some party, registers the* **Waiter**'s *order with a nod, and continues off.*

Alice   The young girl with the frightened eyes was nice. Yes. No beauty, mind you, but very nice. A young woman. She took them back to their son's flat and packed his things. All done in silence, more or less. No, in silence. They sat there. Well, what was there to say? 'Has the earth stopped turning?' 'Day turned into night?' Sensible flat shoes, glimpses of her midriff, reaching for things. She knew where everything was, she was familiar with the place. Nineteen, twenty? Even woman to woman, these days it was difficult to tell. She should have asked her would she like to keep something, the books, a gesture to the young woman. Oh well, never mind, she has her name and address, too, in her bag, if she, if she . . . *(She loses the thought.)* Whatever.

Waitress *has arrived to clear the table, tray clapped under her arm.*

Waitress *(whispers)*   Missus?

Alice *(absently)*   Thank you. Leave the wine. *(She is looking in the direction of the young men's table.)*

Waitress *loads plates / things on top of each other.*

Alice   They've gone. That didn't take them long.

Waitress (*another whisper*)   Missus? (*She has slid into* **Bill***'s chair; she is perhaps still holding her tray; she is leaning forward, in a familiar way, and smiling gently.*) I have to tell someone. My sister-in-law, a lovely woman, had a baby fourteen months ago. She rejected the baby, a lovely woman, she couldn't help it. So my husband and myself took the baby and kept him for over a year. I wouldn't ever run down anybody's child but that baby was the best, we loved him as much if not more than any of our own. More than words can say. We gave him back last Thursday. She killed him two days ago. I had to tell someone.

And she has risen, two clean movements and she has loaded the tray, smiles, bows, as usual, and is gone.

Another break in the buzz of sound for another annoucement. **Alice** *just sits there.*

Bill *is returning accompanied by an* **Official** *in an airport / airline uniform.* **Official** *is giving a document to* **Bill***, which* **Bill** *will sign at some point and return to* **Official***.*

Bill   The, the hearse and limousine are ready on the, the . . .

Official   Tarmac.

Bill   So, so, everything is in order.

Official (*to* **Alice**)   Deepest sympathy.

Alice*'s mind is elsewhere.* (*On* **Waitress***. And, perhaps, also, on* **Bill***.*)

Official   You could have, of course, waited in the VIP lounge.

Alice   No

Official   Had you wanted to, of course.

Bill   Thank you.

Official   Thank you. I'll be at my desk downstairs to escort you on to the tarmac whenever you're ready. (*He goes.*)

Bill   Well, we're ready, aren't we?

He picks up the bill, which is on the table and produces his wallet. He is about to summon **Waitress**, *who has returned to her station.*

Alice   No. Pay him.

She means **Waiter**, *who is about somewhere or who is about to enter. And* **Bill** *joins* **Waiter** *and leaves with him, as to settle the bill.*

Alice *inhales: a long, silent 'O'. Perhaps it is the first satisfactory breath she has drawn in a long time. Then:*

Alice   And the woman does not know what further to say, but she is crying. She hopes that her beloved son and that nice young woman with the frightened eyes slept together, that they'd been warm. She loves that young woman. She loves her husband dearly. And she loves the waitress, Stella, and clings to her for a moment in sympathy and in gratitude for releasing this power within her.

She goes to **Waitress** – '*Excuse me.' They take each other's hand, then embrace for a couple of moments. And, as* **Alice** *leaves,* **Waitress**, *too, is leaving to attend someone requiring her.*